DATABASE DESIGN AND IMPLEMENTATION

DATABASE DESIGN AND IMPLEMENTATION

Shouhong Wang
Hai Wang

Universal-Publishers
Boca Raton

Database Design and Implementation

Universal-Publishers
Boca Raton, Florida
USA • 2011

ISBN-10: 1-61233-015-0
ISBN-13: 978-1-61233-015-0

www.universal-publishers.com

Credit: ORACLE, MySQL are trademarks of Oracle Corporation. IBM DB2 is a trademark of IBM. Windows, Microsoft SQL Server, Microsoft Office, Microsoft Access, Microsoft Excel, and MicrosoftVisual Studio are trademarks of Microsoft Corporation.

Table of Contents

** Electronic teaching material for this textbook includes model syllabus, answers to all assignment questions, sample exams, answers of the exams, lecture PPT, the Microsoft Access database for the textbook SQL examples, Microsoft Access database for Technical Guide II, and others.

PREFACE

Data are valuable assets of the organization. Database is a key component of the information systems in business. Database design is parallel with business process analysis and design for the information system development. This book is designed for business students who study database for information system implementation and data resource management.

IT has been the most innovative field in the modern era. Ironically, after it was first introduced to the computational world longer than three decades ago, the relational database model is still the most popular database model in the IT industry. Although research into object-oriented database has been carrying on for many years, the relational database model is still the main stream of databases, and there is no evidence that the relational database model will phase-out any soon.

Database management systems are powerful tools for constructing and accessing databases. Currently, many user-friendly end-user oriented relational database management systems are available on the commercial software market or are accessible as open source software products. However, people often do not fully realize the importance of the accurate concepts of database. In fact, a poorly designed database or misuse of database management systems can do more harm than good for the organization. The objective of this book is to help students understand the precise concepts of database and develop practical skills of database design and implementation. Upon the completion of study of this book, students should be able to build and to manage databases in a professional manner. More importantly, students should be able to develop their independent learning ability to learn advanced features of database design, implementation, utilization, and management.

There have been hundreds textbooks of database on the market. Given the long history of database, many database textbooks were written decades ago and were revised for numerous times. The volumes of those database textbooks are usually huge since they contain many secondary contents which might be useful decades ago but are no longer essential to know today. On the other hand, contemporary topics, such as physical database design and database application for business intelligence (e.g., OLAP) are lacking in those textbooks. Furthermore, some textbooks are totally database management systems independent, but others seem to over-emphasize specific database management systems (e.g., Oracle or Microsoft Access). This book maintains a good balance between the core concepts and secondary concepts, and includes both basic knowledge of database and hands-on material for Microsoft Access which is a widely available end-user oriented relational database management system. In this book, a huge amount of material about database design, implementation, and application is boiled down to a practically workable volume.

The book is self-contained. It is organized as follows. Chapter 1 provides an overview of database systems. It highlights the key difference between data, information, and knowledge, as well as the concept of data redundancy. Chapter 2 introduces important data structure techniques that are commonly used in databases. Chapter 3 describes the entity-relationship model which is a key element of the foundation of database design. Chapter 4 discusses the relational database model. It ties the entity-relationship model with the relational database model. Chapter 5 details the normalization process which is another key element of the foundation of database design. Chapter 6 explains SQL, a standard database processing language. Chapter 7 discusses the concept and major techniques of physical database design which is critical for vary large scale databases. Chapter 8 discusses major database administration functions. Chapter 9 discusses the key concept of distributed databases in the Internet environment. Chapter 10 discusses the application of relational databases in data warehouse. The book also contains a comprehensive set of student study guides, including Technical Guide I for thorough process of data normalization and ER diagram construction; Technical Guide II for database implementation through using Microsoft Access; answers to selected exercise questions; review sheets for preparation for exams; and a set of PPT slides handouts.

In summary, this textbook is to teach university students in all majors who like to learn database for data resource management in business.

Shouhong Wang, PhD
University of Massachusetts Dartmouth

Hai Wang, PhD
Saint Mary's University

CHAPTER 1. INTRODUCTION

1.1. Data Are Resource of the Organization

Data are valuable resource of the organization. Data can be used for the organization in day-to-day operations as well as in developing competitive advantages. There are many types of data in business. For the time being, no commonly accepted taxonomy of data is available, but the following types of data can be readily observed in business organizations.

- Master data (e.g., customers)
- Transaction data (e.g., sales)
- Historical data (e.g., credit history)
- Secondary data (e.g., industrial publication)
- Subjective data (e.g., end-user survey)

Master data characterize the stakeholders or properties of the organization. They are resident in the system permanently, and are usually used for daily activities. Transaction data record transactions of business, and are usually temporary. They might be kept in the system for a certain period for specific purposes such as auditing. Historical data are chronicle records of useful facts. Secondary data are facts obtained from outside sources. Subjective data are human opinions.

One of the critical issues of data resource management is **data quality**. Generally, data quality is measured by many attributes of data, including accuracy, objectivity, believability, reputation, access, security, relevancy, value-added, timeliness, completeness, amount of data, interpretability, ease of understanding, concise representation, and consistent representation. The ultimate objective of databases is to provide quality data for the organization in these data quality attributes.

1.2. Data, Information, Knowledge

Although the distinction between **data**, **information**, and **knowledge** can never be unambiguous, we must differentiate the three for this database course. For our purpose, data are raw facts; information is a product of processed data; and knowledge is human interpretation of the real world. While tacit knowledge is in the human's mind, explicit knowledge can be represented and stored by computers in a form of information. For instance, sales figures are data which record the facts of sales. *"The total of sales"* is information because it is not a raw fact, but is a processed result of sales of all sales teams and/or over a certain period. A proposition such as *"the low total of sales is a result of the slow economy"* is knowledge, because it is not a raw fact, nor an immediate product of processed data, but is a human perception and judgment. Note that databases discussed in this book store data only, but not information, nor explicit knowledge. Certainly, a computer can always store information and explicit knowledge, but not in the form of database discussed this course. In fact, "information repository" and "knowledge base" are ambiguous terms for less structured digitalized resources.

1.3. Data Redundancy

One of the major objectives of database is to control data redundancy. Data redundancy not only waste resources for data entry and updating, but also causes data inconsistence and thus corrupts the database. For instance, suppose a customer with a certain customer number has filed her name in two store branches of a retail company, and the customer changes her name. The system must remember to change the two names in the two branches. If only one name is changed and the other remains unchanged, then the two names are no longer consistent for the retail company. We will further discuss problems caused by data redundancy later in this book.

Data redundancy occurs when the same **fact** is stored in more than one place. Note that this definition of data redundancy should not be read like "the same number (or text) is stored in more than one place." Let us examine the examples in Figure 1.1 to understand more about data redundancy. There are two cases in Figure 1.1, and both show the storages of the customers' data and purchase data. In case (a), the customer's data repeat in several places. The **fact** that customer 123456 is Smith who lives in Westport Rd. with phone number 508999 is stored twice. Hence, case (a) is a case of data redundancy. In case (b), the **fact** that customer 123456 is Smith is stored in the CUSTOMER table only once. Thus, it does not have the data redundancy problem as occurred in case (a). Take a look at the PURCHASE table in case (b). The same customer number 123456 is stored in the two places. Does data redundancy occur here? The answer is no, because the same customer number 123456 represents the two different **facts** in the two places; that is, the customer 123456 had two purchases. Take a look at both tables in case (b). The same customer number 123456 is stored in both tables. Does data redundancy occur here? The answer is no. In the CUSTOMER table, this number represents the **fact** that customer 123456 is Smith. However, in the PURCHASE table, customer number 123456 represents different **facts** that the customer made purchases.

CUSTOMER- PURCHASE

CustomerNumber	CustomerName	CustomerAddress	CustomerPhone	Purchase	PurchaseTime
123456	Smith	Westport Rd.	508999	$200	10/20/2010 09:45am
234562	Green	Eastport Ave.	509343	$300	10/23/2010 01:32pm
123456	Smith	Westport Rd.	508999	$150	11/08/2010 05:04pm

(a) Data redundancy occurs

CUSTOMER

CustomerNumber	CustomerName	Customer Address	CustomerPhone
123456	Smith	Westport Rd.	508999
234562	Green	Eastport Ave.	509343

PURCHASE

CustomerNumber	Purchase	PurchaseTime
123456	$200	10/20/2010 09:45am
234562	$300	10/23/2010 01:32pm
123456	$150	11/08/2010 05:04pm

(b) There is no data redundancy if the data are stored in this form

Figure 1.1. Data Redundancy

This example shows that a system can avoid data redundancy, as long as the data are stored in an appropriate way. On the other hand, this example also shows potential problems of no-redundancy. For instance, more likely, the user of the data prefers the integrated data as shown in case (a) of Figure 1.1 to find all associated facts in just one table. In this situation, the user has to search the two tables in case (b) and merge them together every time she wants to obtain the integrated data. If the organization has a huge number of tables, it is impossible for human to perform such tedious jobs. This example explains why computerized database systems are needed for data resource management.

1.4. Database and Database System

Organizations use database systems to manage data efficiently and effectively in the following aspects.

(1) Controlled data redundancy - All data files are integrated into a single logical structure of database. In principle, any fact is recorded once.

(2) Data consistency - As a result of data redundancy control, data in database are consistent.

(3) Data sharing - All authorized users in the organization share the data in the database.

(4) Facilitate application development - A database system provides powerful abilities to access the data in the database.

(5) Wide-ranging data management functions - Database management systems provide integrity control, backup and recovery, and security and privacy control functions.

Key terms of database system are explained as follows:
- **Database (DB)** - A database is a collection of data which is accessed by more than one person and/or which is used for more than one purpose.
- **Database management system (DBMS)** - A database management system is a collection of procedures, languages and programs which can be used to facilitate the design, implementation, operation, and maintenance of database systems.
- **Data model** - The data model of a database is the logical structure of data items and

their relationships.

- **Database administration procedures** - An organization with effective management must have the formal policies and procedures for data resource management.
- **Database system** - A database system consists of computer software (DBMS), hardware, **database administrator (DBA)**, database administration procedures, and the database.

The general architecture of a database system is illustrated in Figure 1.2.

1.5. Database Management Systems

To create and manage a database, a **database management system (DBMS)** must be used. A DBMS is a software system which can be used to facilitate the design, implementation, operation, and maintenance of database systems. The key concepts of DBMS and common functions of DBMS are discussed as follows. Note that individual DBMS has its own algorithms and procedures to support those functions at its own sophistication level.

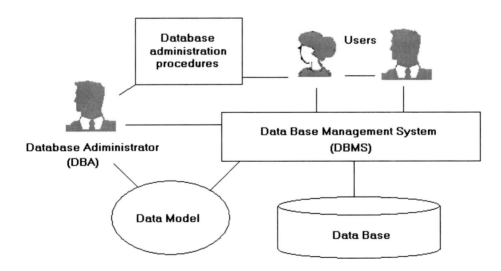

Figure 1.2. Database System

1.5.1. Support database construction and data access

The DBMS provides the **interface** between the user and the computer to allow the user to create a database, to input data, to update the database, and to access the data.

1.5.2. Control data redundancy

In principle, there should be no data redundancy in a database. However, in a large database, no redundancy will result in poor performance (i.e., slow response). As explained later, a large database might have controlled data redundancy. Such data redundancy might be temporary and has a limited scale. One of the DBMS jobs is to ensure the controlled data redundancy does not compromise data **accuracy** and **integrity**.

1.5.3. Provide data integration

Data **integration** refers to the ability to tie together pieces of related data upon the request from the user. For instance, the user might want to know *"what courses John Smith has taken, and the grades he has received from those courses, and who were the instructors of those courses."* One of the DBMS jobs is to support data integration by assembling whatever data available in the database for the user. Usually, integrated data contain data redundancy, and are not supposed to be stored in the database permanently.

1.5.4. Maintain data independency

Data are processed by computer programs. On the other hand, the format of data and the way in which the data are stored on the media (disks) are highly dependent on the individual database. One of the DBMS jobs is to ensure the data **independency** so that any changes in the data storage within the database do not require changes in the application computer programs.

1.5.5. Monitor and improve data retrieval performance

As will be explained later, performance in a large database is crucial for the success of the information system, and must be taken into account for **physical database design**. The DBMS monitors the data retrieval performance and provides information for the DBA for database physical design. A good DBMS has the capacity to support database physical design, or even automatically take actions to improve data retrieval performance. We will further discuss physical database design in Chapter 7.

1.5.6. Control data security

Data security is an important issue of database. The DBMS acts as a security guard for the database. **Authentication** is the process through the DBMS to verify that only registered users are allowed to access the database. **Authorization** management includes all activities of the DBMS to enforce security and privacy of the data. For instance, the DBMS authorizes who is allowed to read, or to change, or to delete, what piece of data.

1.5.7. Enforce business rules and maintain data integrity

Many **business rules** related to the data can be built-in the database through defining cardinality, modality, data access security, etc. For instance, *"one professor can have only one office"* is a business rule. If the DBA builds this business rule in the database through the definition of the cardinality, the DBMS will not allow the database to have a contradictory fact.

Data integrity means **consistency**; that is, there is no conflicting fact in the database. **Data accuracy** and **verifiability** are exchangeable terms of data integrity.

A redundant data set often causes **data anomaly** and violates data integrity. We will further explain data anomaly in Chapter 5. The DBMS eliminates the data redundancy and avoids data anomaly.

1.5.8. Manage concurrency control

When multiple users access and update the same piece of data concurrently, the data could become incorrect. This is caused by the time delays between the data access and the data updating among the multiple users, which is known as the **concurrency** problem. A sophisticated DBMS has advanced techniques and procedures, called concurrency control protocols, to manage concurrency control to ensure correct and prompt data access and data updating by multiple users in the data sharing environment.

1.5.9. Perform backup and recovery

Databases are vulnerable and could be damaged by fire, flood, earthquake, and other human-made or natural disaster. A good DBMS is able to perform **backup** from time to time automatically, and to provide instructions for **recovery** when the database is damaged. We will further explain backup and recovery later in this book.

1.5.10. Maintain data dictionary

A database has a **data dictionary**, as further explained later in Chapter 8. A data dictionary contains data about the database. The DBMS maintains the data dictionary for the data resource management.

1.5.11. Facilitate database restructuring

The business environment keeps changing, so does the database. DBMS facilitates offloading, redefinition, reloading, conversion, etc. to accommodate the changes.

1.6. Commonly Used DBMS for Relational Database

There are many commonly used DBMS for relational database in business.

(1) ORACLE is Oracle Corporation's product. It first appeared around 1979, and was one of the first relational DMBS in the IT industry. It has been widely used in business since then.

(2) IBM DB2 (or DB2) is IBM's product. It was also a pioneer of relational DBMS in the early 1980's. DB2 is considered by many that it is the first database product to use SQL which was also developed by IBM.

(3) MySQL was released in 1995. Later, MySQL becomes open-source software under the GNU General Public License (GPL). MySQL is a popular choice of database for use in Web applications, because it is closely tied to the popularity of PHP, an open-source server-side programming language.

(4) Microsoft SQL Server was Microsoft's entry to the enterprise-level database market, competing against ORACLE and IBM DB2 in about 1989. It is a widely used DBMS in many enterprises.

(5) Microsoft Access was released in 1992 as an end-user oriented DBMS in the Microsoft Office suite. Microsoft Access is easy for end-users to create their own queries, forms and reports, etc., but does not support many sophisticated database management functions. Microsoft Access is well suited for individual and small workgroup use across a network. Generally accepted limits are solutions with 1 GB or less of data (although Access supports up to 2 GB) and up-to 5 simultaneous users.

This textbook uses Microsoft Access as the DBMS for the SQL examples and the technical guides for the course projects of database development and application. This is because (a) Microsoft Access possesses essential features of relational DBMS; (b) It is easy to use for database beginners; (c) It is available virtually everywhere. However, since it is an end-user oriented DBMS and is usually used for small scale databases, Microsoft Access does not support physical database design. Hence, the concepts of physical database design and distributed database design covered in this textbook are unable to be applied to Microsoft Access.

Chapter 1 Exercises

1.* Give examples of master data, transaction data, historical data, secondary data, and subjective data for a student information system (e.g., the Student Information System on the campus).

2. Use examples to explain the differences between data, information, and knowledge.

3. Discuss data redundancy and the solution. What are the advantages and disadvantages of each of the two cases presented in Figure 1.1?

4. Discuss the framework of database systems in Figure 1.2.

5. Discuss the major functions of DBMS.

---

* The questions marked with (*) across the textbook are used for class exercise and discussion. Their answers are listed at the end of the textbook.

CHAPTER 2. DATA STRUCTURE TECHNIQUES FOR DATABASE

This chapter provides an overview of basic data structure techniques used in computer data processing. These basic techniques are used by database management systems at the data physical placement and search level. The purpose of learning these techniques in this course is to understand how the computer can retrieve the needed data speedily through the database management system.

2.1. Data Secondary Storage - Disk

Because CPU memory is limited and volatile, computer programs and data must be stored on secondary storage. There are many forms of secondary storage, including paper, magnetic tape, magnetic disk, flash disk, and optical disk. Magnetic disk is still the most commonly used second storage media in databases. As illustrated in Figure 2.1, the disk read/write device is able to locate an **address** with the track number and sector number of a particular disk to record or to read a piece of data. A collection of all disk surfaces of a disk group with the same track number is called a **cylinder**. All data on the same cylinder can be accessed quickly without moving the read/write heads. Usually, related data are clustered on cylinders for fast access.

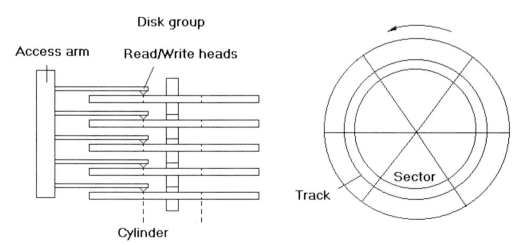

Figure 2.1. Disk

Regardless how fast the disk group spins and how quickly the access arm moves, the speed of data storing and data access on disks is very slow in comparison with that in the CPU. If the data set is huge and the organization of the data set is not well designed, it might take a prohibitive time to retrieve needed data from the disk.

2.2. File, Record, Attribute, and Key

Logically, data are organized into a hierarchy structure in the traditional file systems, as illustrated in Figure 2.2. Database inherits the concept of file systems in many aspects.

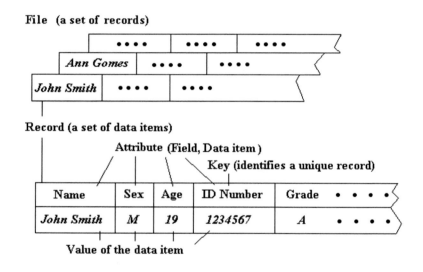

Figure 2.2. File, Record, Attribute, and Key

● **File**: a collection of a set of records. Note that, the term file is often overloaded. For example, a computer program is stored on disk as a "file." However, in this book, we use file exclusively for **data file**, but not computer program file.

● **Record**: a description of a single transaction or entity in a data file. A record is a collection of a set of data items. Normally, record is the unit of data storage on the disk.

• **Attribute,** or **Data Item**, or **Field**: a record has its structure of attributes. Attribute, field, and data item are interchangeable terms.

• **Key**: a data item, or a group of data items, that identifies a unique record in a file.

• **Data**: individual fact; the occurrence or the value of a data item.

2.3. Pointer

To link two remote pieces of data on the disk to allow the computer to trace the sequence, a **pointer** is used. A pointer is attached to the predecessor and contains the address of the successor. Figure 2.3 illustrates the concept of pointer.

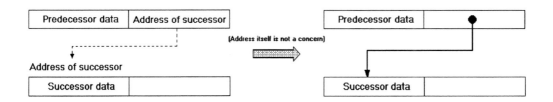

Figure 2.3. Pointer

2.4. Basic File Organizations

Because data retrieval from a disk is much slower than data retrieval from the CPU, the way how data are organized on the disk is crucial for speeding data process. There are three basic file organizations, as discussed below.

2.4.1. Sequential file

The simplest organization of disk file is sequential file. In a **sequential file** (see Figure 2.4), records are stored in physically adjacent locations on the storage medium.

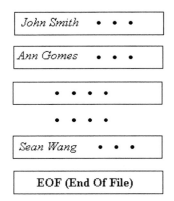

Figure 2.4. Sequential File

In order to find a particular record, the computer has to search the file by checking the records one by one, starting at the beginning of the file, until it finds the desired one, or reaches EOF (End of File) in the case where the search fails. Also, insertion and deletion of records are difficult in a sequential file.

Advantages of sequential files:
(1) Saves space.
(2) No record key is required.
(3) Efficient when all of the records are sequentially processed (e.g. payroll processing for each employee record).

Disadvantages of sequential files:
(1) It would take a long time to find a particular record in random search.
(2) It is difficult to update. For example, it is difficult to insert a record.

2.4.2. Random file

A **random file** organization allows immediate and direct access to individual records in a file. The essence of random accessing is the ability to quickly produce an address from a record's key. The fundamental component of data access in the random file organization is the conversion of the record key of a record to the address of the record on the disk though a formula called **hashing function**. In the general form,

Record key value | Hashing Function $>$ **Address of record on the disk**

In order to explain the feature of hashing functions, we give a simplified example. In this example, the hashing function is defined to be

Address of Record = Remainder of [Record Key / 111]

Suppose there is a record with its Record Key = 4567. Then,

Address of Record = Remainder [4567 / 111]= 16

That is, this record (its key value = 4567) is stored at the location with the address 16. Next time, if one wants to find a record with the key=4567, then the computer will quickly calculate the address according to the hashing function and immediately find it at this address.

In fact, hashing functions used in real systems are much more complicated than this simplified example. No matter how sophisticated a hashing function is, there always exist **synonyms**, or **conflicts**; that is, several key values will be mapping onto the same address. For example, suppose the above example hashing function is applied, the data system has three records, and their key values are 4567, 1126, 349, respectively. According to the hashing function, all the three records should be placed at address 16, which is impossible.

Key   4567 $\rightarrow$ Address 16
Key   1126 $\rightarrow$ Address 16
Key   349 $\rightarrow$ Address 16

Such a problem can happen frequently especially the data file is large. To solve this problem, an overflow area is created on the disk to hold conflicting records. The pointer technique is then used to trace all conflicting records. Figure 2.5 briefly illustrates the solution. For instance, suppose the record with key value 4567 is stored on the disk first, and occupies the address 16. Later, the record with key value 1126 comes in. Because of the conflict, it is placed to the overflow area at any unoccupied address, say 100. The system updates the pointer of the first record with key value 4567 to 100. Next time when searching the record with key value 1126, the computer uses the hashing function and locates address 16 first. Because the located record has an unwanted key value, the computer then follows the pointer to trace the conflict records until the record with key value 1126 is found, or "null" is reached which means a failure. Obviously, when the data file is huge, the random file organization is not an ideal option.

Advantages of random files:
(1) It can randomly access an individual record very fast, if there are only few synonyms.
(2) It is efficient in updating (e.g., adding and modifying records).

Disadvantages of random files:
(1) Sequential access is impossible.
(2) A record key is necessary.
(3) Wastes spaces.
(4) Synonyms make search slow.

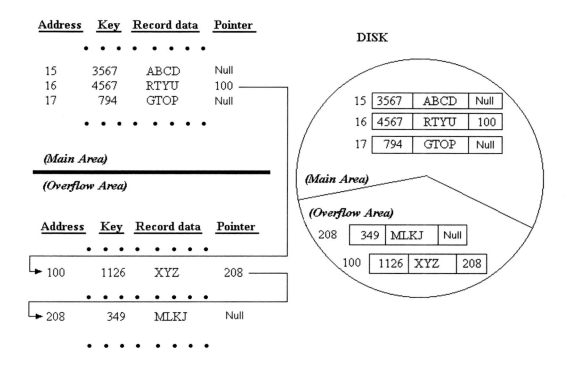

Figure 2.5. Conflict and Its Solution in Random Files

2.4.3. Indexed file

An **indexed file** keeps an index table which associate record keys with addresses. An index table is comparable to a table of contents in a textbook (see Figure 2.6). When a record is stored, it can be placed anywhere as long as the disk space is available, and then the index table is updated by adding its key and the address. In fact, the index table is a set of pointers.

Index Table

Record Key	Address of Record
3081	1010
4123	0239
1056	4320
• • • •	• • • •

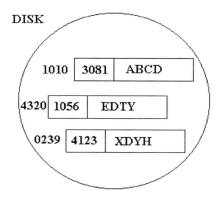

Figure 2.6. Index Table in an Indexed File

Usually, an index table is small and can be manipulated in the CPU memory. Hence, the conversion of a record key to the address of the record takes little time. Given a record key, the computer can find the record on the disk almost directly. Also, an index table may be sorted based on a sequence of the record key values if needed. Indexed files are generally good for random access, sequential processing, and file updating such as record insertion and deletion. Generally, index tables can also be designed for non-key attributes.

However, if a data file is extremely large, then its index table will be so large that the index table has to be placed on the disk. Then the index table itself becomes a sequential disk file which is poor for random search. This type of indexed file organization is called **linear indexed file** because of this property.

Advantages of indexed files:
(1) It can be used in both sequential and random access. Processing speed is fairly good for both, if the indexed file is not extremely huge.
(2) It is efficient in adding a record, sorting and updating the file, if the indexed file is not extremely huge.

Disadvantages of indexed files:

(1) A record key is necessary.

(2) If the data file is huge, then the linear index table becomes a sequential disk file, and processing will be slow.

2.5. B-tree

2.5.1. Overview of B-tree

A **B-tree** is a hierarchical structure with multiple index records. B-trees overcome the disadvantages of simple linear indexed file organization and improve the performance of search in very large databases. There are many variants of B-tree. Although it has been with us for a quite long time, the concept of B-tree techniques still dominates the modern database systems. In fact, a large database is supported by massive B-trees.

Figure 2.7 shows an example of B-tree. As you can see in the figure, a B-tree consists of index records which organized into a reverse-tree. The tree has one index record on the top, which is called root. The tree can have many levels. In the example of Figure 2.7, the B-tree has only two levels. An index records at the bottom level is called leaf. The index records in a B-tree are of the same format. Each index record has a certain number of pairs that hold a key value and a pointer. In this example, the number of key-value-pointer pairs is 4. Suppose the data system has 8 cylinders, and each cylinder has records with a range of key values as illustrated in Figure 2.7. In the example of Figure 2.7, there are three index records at the leaf level. The first leaf index record uses three key-value-pointer pairs to link itself to the first three cylinders in such a way that each key-value-pointer pair keeps the maximum key value of the records on each cylinder and the address of the corresponding cylinder. The other two leaf index records have the similar connections with the rest five cylinders. To build a tree, higher level index records are needed to link themselves to the leaf index records. In this example, because each index record has 4 key-value-pointer pairs and only 3 leaf index records exist at the leaf level, only one index record at the next higher level is needed. In this case, this index record becomes the root of the tree. In the root index record, three key-value-pointer pairs are used to link itself to the lower level index records in such a way that each key-value-pointer pair keeps the maximum key value of the lower level index record and the address of the corresponding lower level index record.

In principle, the computer keeps the root of the B-tree in CPU in order to use the B-tree. We use the example in Figure 2.7 to explain how a B-tree can help data retrieval quickly. Suppose we want to find the data of the record with the key value 6000. The computer starts from the root. Since 3000<6000<6743, the computer uses the second pointer in the root index record to find the second index record at the next level. Since 5123<6000<6743, the computer uses the third pointer in the index record and locates cylinder 6 to find the record. In such a way, the computer uses only two steps to find the needed data record.

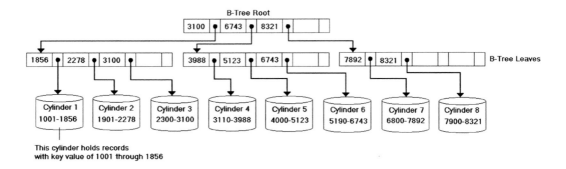

Figure 2.7. An Example of B-Tree

The construction of B-tree applies the following general rules.

(1) A B-tree consists of index records that are organized into a tree. The tree has its root with one and just one index record on the top, and a number of levels.

(2) Each index record accommodates the same number of pairs (4 in the example of Figure 2.7), and each pair can hold a key-value and a pointer.

(3) Each index record is at least half full (in the example of Figure 2.7, at least 2 pairs in an index record are occupied with key-values and pointers, and the rest pairs can be empty).

(4) In each occupied key-value-pointer pair, the pointer points to an index record at the next level or a disk cylinder, and the key-value is the maximum key value in the

pointed index record or the maximum key value on the cylinder.

Other than the four rules, the construction of a B-tree can be flexible, depending on the situation, or arbitrations. For example, the B-tree constructor (the DBMS if not human) determines how many index records are used, how many levels the tree has, whether an index record should have empty key-value-point pairs, etc. depending on the case.

In fact, a large database has a large number of large-scale B-trees. The computer constructs and maintains these large-scale B-trees to make the random access efficient.

2.5.2. B-tree maintenance

Data might be added or deleted from the cylinders, and the B-tree has to be updated correspondingly. Follow the example in Figure 2.7. Figure 2.8(a) shows a simple case of B-tree updating when Cylinder 6 is full and a new cylinder (Cylinder 9) must be added to accommodate additional records with key values between 5190 and 6743. In this case, split the records on Cylinder 6 arbitrarily and move a part of the records to Cylinder 9. As there is an empty pair in the index record, the computer simply adds a key-value-pointer pair to the index record.

Follow the example in Figure 2.8(a). Figure 2.8(b) shows a little complicated case when Cylinder 5 also happens to be full after Cylinder 9 has been added. To accommodate additional records with key values between 4000 and 5123, a new cylinder (Cylinder 10) must be added. However, as the index record has been full, it must be split into two index records, and each index record must have at least two key-value-pointer pairs (i.e., at least a half of pairs are occupied). It is not important whether one index record has two pairs or three pairs, as long as the splitting follows the construction rules. As the low level of the B-tree has been changed, the upper level of the B-tree (in this case, the root) has to be updated correspondingly, as shown in Figure 2.8(b).

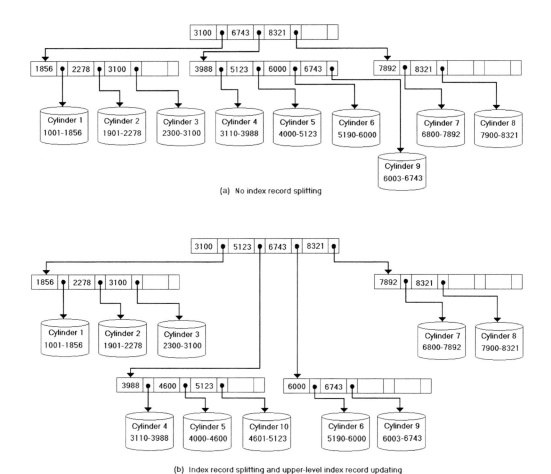

(a) No index record splitting

(b) Index record splitting and upper-level index record updating

Figure 2.8. B-Tree Updating in Response to Data Insertion

Several points are worth thinking further.

(1) A data deletion may also trigger B-tree updating, although it might not be necessary.

(2) In Figure 2.8(b), the root index record of the B-tree is full. If the data set keeps growing and more and more new cylinders are added, eventually the root index record

has to be split into two index records. Then, the B-tree must grow by creating a new root above the two index records.

(3) In our examples, the B-tree is used for indexing key values. Actually, B-trees can also be used for non-keys.

(4) A database management system can construct and maintain a huge number of B-trees so that random data access would be efficient. On the other hand, significant computational resource would be devoted to the B-tree construction and maintenance.

(5) Can the B-tree avoid splitting the index records by moving key-value-pointer pairs around? For instance, following the case of the B-tree in Figure 2.8(a), suppose Cylinder 5 is full, and is split. Cylinder 10 is going to be added. Can one move the key-value-pointer pair for Cylinder 9 to the unoccupied space in the index record for Cylinders 7 and 8? To answer this question, you need to imagine that a B-tree is usually huge. If one keeps moving key-value-pointer pairs around, eventually every index record of the B-tree becomes full. At that point, just one data insertion will cause reconstruction of the entire huge B-tree which is the worst case for the B-tree maintenance. Thus, it is a good practice to split the index record when it has no room for an additional cylinder. In such a way, the B-tree maintenance job consumes only tiny computational resource each time.

(6) B-tree is good for random search. In cases where a sequential search occurs, the search process starts from the root and ends with the leaf repeatedly, which is not efficient. To improve the search performance for sequential searches, a variation of B-tree called B+-tree technique has been used. In B+-trees, there are pointer-links between the leaf index records (i.e., the index records at the lowest level).

Chapter 2 Exercises

1. A sequential disk file is as follows:

> Linda...
> Jone...
> John...
> Oldman...
> Youngman...
> Mark...
> EOF (End of File)

In order to find the record of Youngman, how many records the computer has to read from the disk? Explain why sequential file is rarely used in a large database.

2. A hashing function is

Address of record = Remainder of [Record key / 19].

Suppose that a record key is 379. What is the address of this record?

3. An indexed file for the inventory data on disk and its index table are as follows:

Disk file

Disk Address	Record			
	Record Key	Item Name	Quantity	Price
43	130	Pen	300	$4
20	12	Paper	200	$5
05	23	Disk	250	$6
10	43	Watch	100	$7
. . . .	. . . .			

Index Table

Record Key	Disk Address
20	14
130	43
43	10
14	29
. . . .	. . . .

What is the data of the record with a key value of 43? Explain the advantages and disadvantages of linear indexed files.

4. In the indexed file organization presented in Question 3, how can the computer read all of the records from the disk logically sequentially based on the values of the record key in the ascending order?

5. In the indexed file organization presented in Question 3, if one wants to randomly read individual records based on the price of the item, how would you design the index table?

6. Construct a B-tree for the file on 9 cylinders of the disk. The highest key values on the 9 cylinders are

Cylinder 1: 1234
Cylinder 2: 2345
Cylinder 3: 3456
Cylinder 4: 4567
Cylinder 5: 5678
Cylinder 6: 6789
Cylinder 7: 7890
Cylinder 8: 8991
Cylinder 9: 9992

a) Each index record has 4 key-value-pointer pairs, and the number of index records at the lowest level of the tree is the minimum.

b) Each index record has 2 key-value-pointer pairs, and the number of index records at the lowest level of the tree is the minimum.

7. Consider the B-tree below. A record has been added to cylinder 6, causing a cylinder split. The empty cylinder is number 20. The highest key value on cylinder 6 is now 5600, and the highest key value on cylinder 20 is now 6000. Update the B-tree.

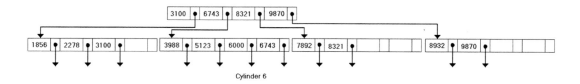

8.* Consider the B-tree as shown below:

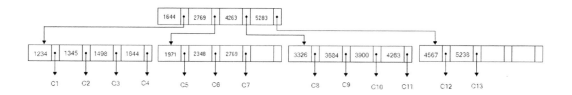

a) A record has just been added to Cylinder 6, causing a cylinder split. The highest key value on Cylinder 6 is now 2111; the highest key value on Cylinder 22, the empty reserve cylinder that received half of Cylinder 6's records is now 2348. Update the tree index accordingly.

b) A record has just been added to Cylinder 10, causing a cylinder split. The highest key value on Cylinder 10 is now 3770; the highest key value on Cylinder 30, the empty reserve cylinder that received half of Cylinder 10's records is now 3900. Update the tree index accordingly.

CHAPTER 3. DATA MODELS

3.1. Overview of Data Models

A data model is a representation of complex data structures and their relationships of the target real world, or the system (e.g., Student Information System), for database design. In the context of systems analysis and design, data modeling is the data-centered analysis in conjunction with process modeling (the process-centered analysis) for the information system development.

To model the data and their relationships, graphics must be used because verbal descriptions are often ambiguous, and thus are difficult to be used for database design.

In principle, a data modeling approach (or the type of graphics) does not necessarily tie with a particular type of database system, but actually it does. In the database history, there have been four major data models, as listed below.

- **Hierarchical model** for hierarchical databases;
- **Network model** for network databases;
- **Entity-relationship (ER)** model for relational databases; and
- **Object-oriented** model for object-oriented databases.

The hierarchical model and hierarchical databases were used in the 1960s. Some legacy information systems might still run those databases. In the hierarchical model, all data are organized into a tree. Due to the limitation of the hierarchical model, the network model was created in the 1970s. The network model describes the data using network charts. However, the network databases were too complicated, and they had not become popular yet when the relational data model was invented. The entity-relationship (ER) model and relational databases were developed in the late 1970s, and still dominate the database area today. Since the early 1990s, the object-oriented model and object-oriented database were developed. The **Unified Modeling Language (UML)**, a set of complicated diagramming methods, was created for the object-oriented model. However, for many reasons, object-oriented databases never became widespread. For the time being, it is unlikely that ER model and relational database will be replaced by something else within a foreseeable time period. Thus, this book focuses on the ER model and relational database.

3.2. The ER Model

The ER model is the most widely accepted model of data for database. Ironically, there is no universally accepted standard for **ER diagram** (**ERD**) notations despite of the popularity of the ER model. Historically, there have been many variations of versions of ERD notations. In fact, none of them is perfect. For database professionals, it does not matter what ERD style is used because they know exactly what a specific notation or symbol means. It has become a norm that people just use whatever ERD style the organization has already adopted. For teaching beginners, it might be ideal to use just one ERD style to avoid confusion. However, as you will see, any single ERD style cannot convey all important points for database design. Accordingly, two ERD styles which are very parallel will be used for this book. In this chapter, we use so-called **logical ERD** first to explain the concept of data modeling. Later, we will transit from the logical ERD to so-called physical ERD. The two styles will convey all essential concepts for database design. More importantly, the conversion of a physical ERD into the relational database will be just one seamless step. Hence, you are recommended to use physical ERD for your assignments and database project.

Generally, the ER model has two key elements: **entity** and **relationship** between entities, as discussed next.

3.3. Entity, Attribute, and Primary Key

An entity is a class of **objects**. There are three major types of entities.

• A **physiomorphic** entity is a class of physically existing objects; e.g., CUSTOMER, STUDENT, and INVENTORY.

• An **event** entity represents a class of events of routine operations; e.g., GAME and CREDIT_APPROVAL.

• A **document** entity is a class of artificial abstractions; e.g., INVOICE.

Each entity has its **attribute**(s) which characterize the entity. For example, a STUDENT entity would be described by student ID, student name, address, etc. Attribute and field are exchangeable terms. An attribute has its **data type**, such as text (character string), integer, decimal number, etc. An **instance** (or **occurrence**) of attribute is called a **value** of the attribute. For example, "John Smith" is a value of attribute StudentName. An attribute can have many **values**. An object with values in all attributes is an **entity instance**. For example, "01234567, John Smith, 286 Westport, 2012" is an instance of STUDENT.

Each entity has its unique **identifier**, called **primary key** or **key** for short. The key of an entity is an attribute or a combination of attributes that can be used to identify the unique object in this class. For example, the attribute StudentID is the key of STUDENT because it is the identifier to find a specific student object.

Figure 3.1 shows an ERD for entity STUDENT. We use the following convention of diagramming notations for entity.

- Use the rectangular shape for entity;
- Use caps for entity name;
- Use the camel style for attribute names – no space;
- Use the asterisk sign (*) to indicate the primary key of the entity.

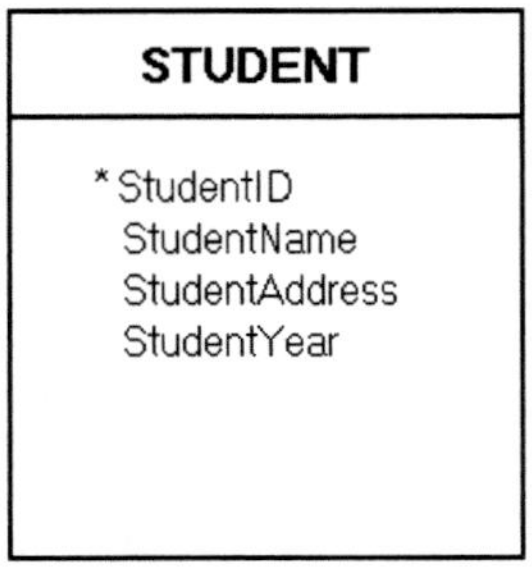

STUDENT
*StudentID StudentName StudentAddress StudentYear

Figure 3.1. An Example of Entity and Attributes in the ER Model

3.4. Relationship

A relationship describes the association among the instances of entities. The diamond shape and a verb phrase are used to represent a relationship in the ERD. Binary, unary, and ternary relationships are the major types of relationships in terms of the number of entities involved, as discussed next.

3.4.1. Binary, unary, ternary relationships

The most common relationships describe associations between the instances of two entities, called **binary relationships**. For example, *Occupy* is a binary relationship between instances of PROFESSOR and OFFICE, representing "*who occupies which office*" (see Figure 3.2). *Use* is a binary relationship between the instances of COURSE and CLASSROOM, representing "*which course uses what classroom*" (see Figure 3.3). *Teach* is a binary relationship between the instances of PROFESSOR and COURSE, representing "*which professor teaches what course*" (see Figure 3.4).

Unary relationships describe association between the instances of the **same** entity. For instance, *Mentoring* is a unary relationship between the instances of PROFESSOR, representing "*who is the mentor of other professors*" (see Figure 3.5). *Prerequisite* is a unary relationship between the instances of COURSE, representing "*which course is a prerequisite of what other courses*" (see Figure 3.6).

Ternary relationships describe association between the instances of three entities. For instance, *Teach* is a ternary relationship between the instances of PROFESSOR, COURSE, and STUDENT, representing "*who teaches what course for which student*" (see Figure 3.7).

Apparently, one may use three binary relationships to describe the relationships between the instances of PROFESSOR, COURSE, and STUDENTS. The difference between three binary relationships and one ternary relationship is significant, and could be complicated if many business rules are involved. Generally, a ternary relationship assumes that the instances of the three entities occurred concurrently, while three binary relationships relax this assumption and make the entire relationships among the instances of the three entities flexible. Because of this, more than 3-ways relationships are uncommon.

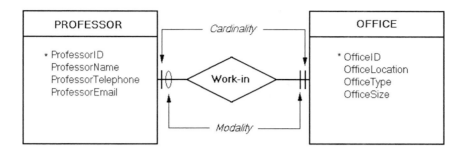

Figure 3.2. Binary One-to-One Relationship

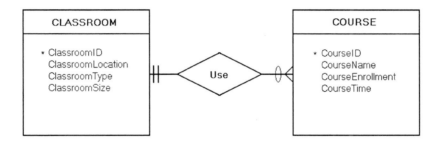

Figure 3.3. Binary One-to-Many Relationship

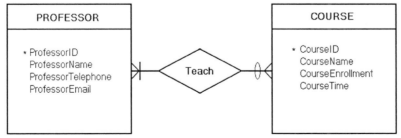

Figure 3.4. Binary Many-to-Many Relationship

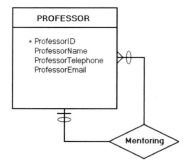

Figure 3.5. Unary One-to-Many Relationship

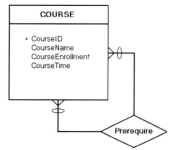

Figure 3.6. Unary Many-to-Many Relationship

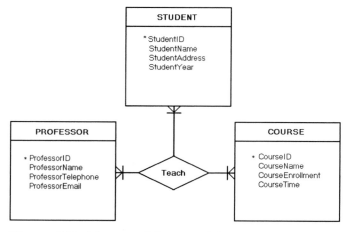

Figure 3.7. Ternary Many-to-Many Relationship

3.4.2. Cardinality

The **cardinality** is attached to a relationship to indicate the maximum number of instances of entities involved in the relationship. There are three types of relationships between the instances of entities in the ER model in terms of cardinality: **one-to-one** (1:1), **one-to-many** (1:M), and **many-to-many** (M:M). The "crow's foot" notations, as shown in Figures 3.2-3.7, represent the cardinalities.

Figure 3.2 is an example of 1:1 relationship between the instances of PROFESSOR and OFFICE, which means *"one professor can occupy at most one office, and one office can be occupied at most one professor."*

Figure 3.3 is an example of 1:M relationship between the instances of CLASSROOM and COURSE, which means *"one classroom can be used for many courses, and one course can use at most one classroom."*

Figure 3.4 shows an example of M:M relationship between the instances of PROFESSOR and COURSE which means *"one professor can teach many courses, and one course can be taught by many professors."*

Figure 3.5 shows an example of 1:M unary relationship between the instances of PROFESSOR which means *"one professor can be a mentor of many professors, and one professor can have at most one mentor."*

Figure 3.6 shows an example of M:M unary relationship between the instances of COURSE which means *"one course can have many prerequisites, and one course can be a prerequisite of many courses."*

Figure 3.7 shows an example of M:M ternary relationship between the instances of PRROFESSOR, STUDENT, and COURSE which means *"one professor can teach many courses for many students, one student can take many courses taught by many professors, and one course can be taught by many professors for many students."* Note that a business rule behind this ternary ER model is that team teaching is allowed in this model.

3.4.3. Modality

The **modality** is the minimum number of instances of entity that can be involved in the relationship. In the ER model, modality can be either 0 or 1. For example, the modality shown in Figure 3.2 means *"one professor can work in at least one office, and one office* *can have no professor (i.e., can be empty).*" Similar to cardinality, modality can be used for the database management system to enforce the pertinent business rules. For instance, in our example, the database will not make a mistake that a professor has no office to work-in.

Several important points about the ER model are worth noting.

(1) The relationships between the instances of entities along with the cardinalities and modalities are not given, but are modeled by the database designer using ER diagrams as a tool. They depend on the **business rules** of the business environment, or the **assumptions** made for the particular database. For instance, in our example, we assume one course can have only one classroom. If this assumption is not true for another database, the 1:M cardinality must be changed correspondingly.

(2) The cardinalities and modalities will be used by the database management system to enforce the pertinent business rules. For instance, in our example, the database will not make a mistake that a professor has two or more offices.

(3) In relational database, there is no way to present M:M relationships directly in the database. Any M:M relationship must be converted into 1:M relationships through the use of **associative entity**, as discussed in detail later in this chapter.

3.5. Instrument for Implementing 1:1 and 1:M Relationships – Foreign Key

In principle, the ER model is applicable for any types of databases. Practically, however, the ER model is intended for relational database. We will discuss relational database in details in Chapter 4. In this section, we discuss the way any relational database implements 1:1 and 1:M relationships, and describe how the ER model represents the implementation of 1:1 or 1:M relationships for the relational database.

To implement a 1:1 or 1:M relationship, a linkage between the entities is needed. The instrument used for the linkage is **foreign key**. A foreign key is the primary key of one entity and "travels" to another entity to implement the linkage. For example, the ER model in Figure 3.2 can be detailed by adding the foreign key *OfficeID* from OFFICE to the PROFESSOR entity, as shown in Figure 3.8. This foreign key represents "*which professor works-in what office.*" In this book, we use *Italic* font for foreign keys. Similarly, the ER model in Figure 3.3 can be detailed by adding the foreign key *ClassroomID* from CLASSROOM to the COURSE entity, as shown in Figure 3.9, to represent *"which course uses what classroom."* Note that the primary key in one table and its corresponding foreign key in another table must have the same **domain of values**; that is, they have the same data type (e.g., both the primary key ClassroomID in CLASSROOM and the foreign key *ClassroomID* in COURSE are designed to be a text string with 7 characters).

Figure 3.10 is the implementation of the unary 1:M relationship in Figure 3.5. Note that, within an entity, no two attributes can share the same attribute name. Hence, a different foreign key name, say, *MentorID*, is created for the foreign key.

It is an important fact that the 1:1 and 1:M relationships which are explicitly annotated in the ERD do not have their independent body inside the relational database other than foreign keys. In other words, 1:1 and 1:M relationships are represented by the relational database implicitly through foreign keys. Because of this, some styles of ERD even do not include relationship diamond symbols.

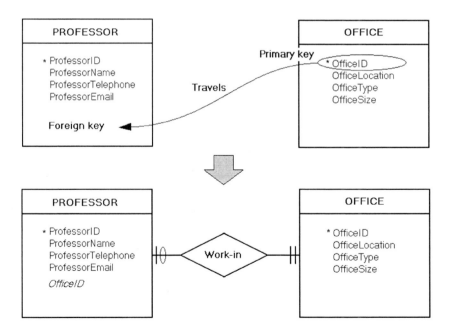

Figure 3.8. Foreign Key (*OfficeID*) Implements the Binary 1:1 Relationship in Figure 3.2

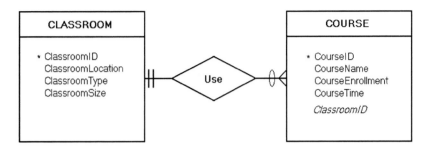

Figure 3.9. Foreign Key (*ClassroomID*) Implements the Binary 1:M
Relationship in Figure 3.3

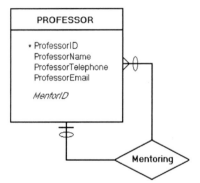

Figure 3.10. Foreign Key (*MentorID*) Implements the Unary 1:M Relationship
in Figure 3.5

While it is worth thinking deeper by yourself why foreign key can implement 1:1 and 1:M relationships and what rules are applied, you need to remember the following rules.

(1) For a 1:1 relationship, you can arbitrarily choose the primary key from either entity and place it as the foreign key to the other entity. For instance, for the 1:1

relationships in Figure 3.2, you may place *ProfessorID* as the foreign key into the OFFICE entity. However, if one of the modalities is 0, it is better to place the foreign key into the entity with the 0 modality, as we did in Figure 3.8. In such a way, the value of the foreign key can never be empty.

(2) For a 1:M relationship, you place the primary key of the entity with the 1 cardinality into the entity with the M cardinality as the foreign key.

(3) The primary key in one table and its corresponding foreign key in another table have the same domain of values.

3.6. Instrument for Implementing M:M Relationships – Associative Entity

To implement an M:M relationship, the instrument is a little more complicated. In the relational database, there is no way to represent an M:M relationship unless an addition entity, called **associative entity**, is created. The associative entity converts the binary M:M relationship into two 1:M relationships which can then be represented in the relational database. For example, the M:M relationship in Figure 3.4 is converted into two 1:M relationships by adding an associative entity, called TEACH in this example.

There are important rules in applying associative entity.

(1) Once an associative entity is introduced, the binary M:M relationship becomes two 1:M relationships, and the associative entity is on the M sides between the two original entities. The original M:M relationship disappears. In the example of Figure 3.11, the original M:M relationship between PROFESSOR and COURSE becomes the combination of the 1:M relationship between PROFESSOR and TEACH and the 1:M relationship between COURSE and TEACH.

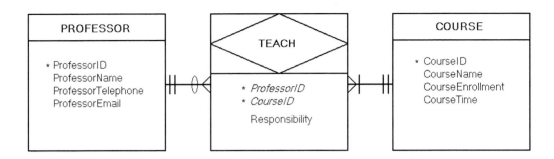

Figure 3.11. Associative Entity Is the Instrument for Implementing the Binary M:M Relationship in Figure 3.4

(2) To distinct an associative entity from an ordinary entity, a diamond symbol is added on the top.

(3) Follow the same rules of implementing 1:M relationships, place the primary key of the entity on the 1 side into the associative entity as the foreign key. If the original M:M relationship is binary, then the associative entity can have two foreign keys. In Figure 3.11, *ProfessorID* and *CourseID* are the foreign keys from PROFESSOR and COURSE, respectively.

(4) Usually, the combination of the foreign keys in the associative entity is the primary key of the associative entity. In Figure 3.11, the **combination primary key** (or simply **combination key**) of TEACH is [*ProfessorID+CourseID*].

(5) There are two variations of setting the primary key for an associative entity.

(a) One might create a new single attribute as the primary key for the associative entity to substitute the tedious combination key. For instance, in the example of Figure 3.11, it is possible to create a new attribute, say, TeachID, as the primary key of TEACH. *ProfessorID* and *CourseID* are no longer a part of primary key, but are still the foreign keys in the associative entity.

(b) One may add an addition attribute(s) to join the combination key. For instance, one may want to add *TeachAssitID* to the associative entity as a part of combination primary key to indicate the uniqueness of an instance of the associative entity. If so, the new combination key will become [*ProfessorID+CourseID+TeachAssitID*].

(6) An associative entity usually has its own attribute(s) that is not a part of either of the original entity but describes the characteristics of the associative entity. Those attributes are called **intersection data**. For example, in Figure 3.11, Responsibility is the intersection data attribute to describe the specific characteristics of the relationship between PROFESSOR and COURSE: *"what is the role (e.g., principle-teacher or co-teacher) of the professor who teaches this course?"*

The above rules can be extended to the unary and ternary relationships. Figure 3.12 is the implementation of the unary M:M relationship in Figure 3.6. Note that, in the unary relationship, the names of the two foreign keys cannot be the same. Thus, *PrerequisiteID* is used for one of the foreign keys. In this example, the associative entity has no intersection data, and just describes *"what course is the prerequisite of what course."*

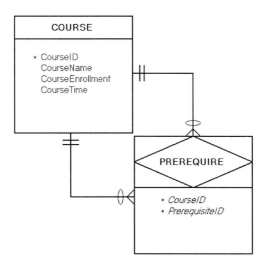

Figure 3.12. Implementation of the Unary M:M Relationship in Figure 3.6

Figure 3.13 is the implementation of the ternary M:M relationship in Figure 3.7. In this example, we add intersection data attribute called Assessment.

As shown in Figure 3.8 through Figure 3.13, in comparison with the logical ERDs in Figure 3.2 through Figure 3.7, the physical ERDs include foreign keys, as well as applicable associative entities and intersection data. Note that there is no explicit M:M relationship in the physical ERDs, because any M:M relationship will eventually be converted into 1:M relationships for the relational database.

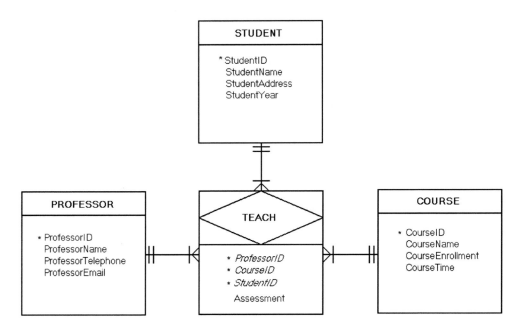

Figure 3.13. Implementation of the Ternary M:M Relationship in Figure 3.7

3.7. Summary of ER Diagram Notations
Figure 3.14 provides a summary of ERD notations that are commonly used in the database field.

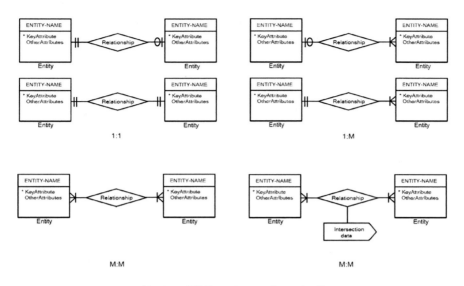

(a)   Logical ER Diagram Notations (Intermediate Tools)

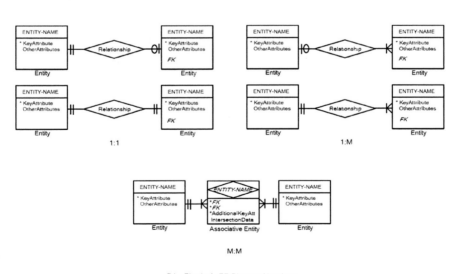

(b)   Physical ER Diagram Notations

Figure 3.14. Summary of ER Diagram Notations

As pointed out earlier in this textbook, there is no standard set of ERD notations. For example, a five-sided box is commonly used for including intersection data for an M:M relationship in logical ERDs. Clearly, Figure 3.14 shows the advantages of the physical ERD in that (a) foreign keys are included; (b) associative entities are presented; and (c) any M:M relationships are converted into 1:M relationships. These properties ensure precise designs of databases. As you will see in Chapter 4, the transition from the physical ERD to the internal model of relational database is just one seamless step. For the database design beginners, the logical version can be a transitional tool for constructing ERD, but the physical ERDs are strongly recommended in order to avoid any errors in database construction.

3.8. Construction of ER Diagram

There are two major starting points for the **database designer** in constructing an **ER diagram**: transcripts of the target real world, and sample datasheets from the target real world.

3.8.1. Transcripts

It is common to use descriptions of the real world for constructing an ERD. A transcript could be a summary of your observations, or records of interviews, or verbal documents of surveys. For instance, we might have the following transcript that describes a school information system.

> *The School wants to create a database to maintain data for the school. Student data should include identification, name, address, and the earliest enrollment year. Professor data should include identification, name phone number, and office. Each professor has her/his own office, and teaches many courses each semester. Several professors might form a team to teach a single course. Each student can take many courses each semester. Course data should include unique course number, title, and enrollment cap. Each course can have its prerequisites. Each course must have a classroom. The school wants to keep track of students' grades.*

Based on the transcript, you might be able to construct an ERD which would look like Figure 3.15. There are several steps you may apply.

(1) Identify entities and their attributes through identifying **nouns**.

(2) Identify relationships through identifying **verbs** or verb phrases.

(3) Identify cardinalities and modalities through identifying **business rules**.

(4) Make commonsensical **assumptions** if the transcript does not provide all information you need for modeling the system using ERD.

(5) Construct a logical ERD for the case.

(6) If there is an M:M relationship in your logical ERD, convert the M:M relationship into 1:M relationships by adding an associative entity along with its intersection data attributes.

(7) Complete the notations for all primary keys and foreign keys.

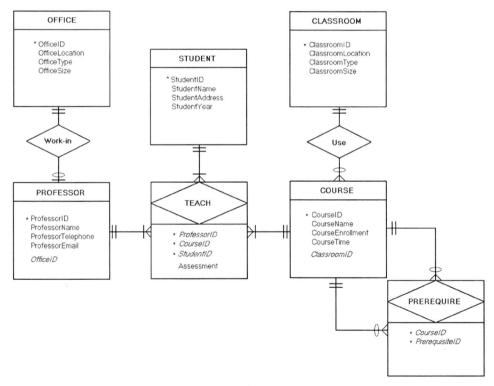

Figure 3.15. ER Diagram Derived from the Transcript

3.8.2. Sample datasheets

Another approach to generating an ERD is to collect sample datasheets from the real world, including business reports, forms, Web sites, etc. The sample datasheets collected are usually organized for particular application purposes and contains redundancy or secondary processed facts (e.g., totals). You need to abstract entities and relationships from those datasheets. For instance, Figure 3.16 shows a sample datasheet that you might have not seen before. As an exercise, you can make an ERD for the datasheet in Figure 3.16.

Department of Decision & Information Sciences		TEACHING SCHEDULE –		Spring 2011			
Instructor's Name:		**Shouhong Wang**		Office Location:		CCB #325	
Office/Conference Hours:		MWF 10:00-10:50 1:00-1:50 3:00-3:50		Telephone Ext.		8579	
		9:00-9:50	**10:00**	**11:00-11:50**	**1:00**	**2:00-2:50**	**3:00**
MON	Course Name Course Number (Section) Room Number	MIS 322 (01) Business Systems Analysis & Design T-201	Office Hours	MIS 212 (01) Programming & Problem Solving CCB-Lab	Office Hours	MIS 432 (01) Database Design & Implementation CCB-Lab	Office Hours
TUES		Research, Teaching innovation, Services					
WED	Course Name Course Number (Section) Room Number	MIS 322 (01) Business Systems Analysis & Design T-201	Office Hours	MIS 212 (01) Programming & Problem Solving CCB-Lab	Office Hours	MIS 432 (01) Database Design & Implementation CCB-Lab	Office Hours
THURS		Research, Teaching innovation, Services					
FRI	Course Name Course Number (Section) Room Number	MIS 322 (01) Business Systems Analysis & Design T-201	Office Hours	MIS 212 (01) Programming & Problem Solving CCB-Lab	Office Hours	MIS 432 (01) Database Design & Implementation CCB-Lab	Office Hours

Figure 3.16. A Sample Datasheet for Construction of ER Diagram

Several rules can be applied to constructing ERD using sample datasheets.

(1) Identify the entities that have their attributes in the datasheet table.

(2) Identify the relationships between the entities based on your understanding of the business environment.

(3) Identify cardinalities and modalities based on commonsensical assumptions that can be applied to the business environment.

(4) Construct a logical ERD for the case.

(5) If there is an M:M relationship in your logical ERD, convert the M:M relationship into 1:M relationships by adding an associative entity along with its intersection data attributes.

(6) Complete the notations for all primary keys and foreign keys.

Apparently, when sample datasheets are used for constructing ERD, more assumptions would be needed. Also, for a real-world database project, it is more likely to use both transcripts and numerous sample datasheets from a variety of application areas.

3.8.3. Iterations of ER diagram construction

Thus far, we have learned how to create an ERD for the database based on verbal descriptions of the system or sample datasheets used in the system. One question you might have in your mind: "*Is there a criterion for judging whether an ER diagram is correct or wrong?*" The answer to this question is "yes." We will return to this question in Chapter 5 on normalization.

The above question tells that, regardless whether the start point of an ERD is system descriptions or is sample datasheets, one-shot construction may not result in a good ERD. The construction of ERD and the normalization process should be carried out together. If an initial ERD is generated before the normalization process, this trial ERD might need to be revised after the normalization process to become the approved ERD. In fact, if the start point is sample datasheets, one may perform the normalization process before constructing a trial ERD for the database. This fine point is illustrated in Technical Guide I in this textbook through an example.

An ERD is the design blueprint for the target database. If the ERD is wrong, the target database based on the flawed ERD must be wrong, and would become a collection of garbage.

Chapter 3 Exercises

1. You are planning to open a motel. A rough sketch of the online reservation form is shown below. Create an ERD for the database that can support the online reservation system, making all necessary commonsensical assumptions.

Online Reservation

Reservation Information

Check-In Date:

Check-Out Date:

Number of Guests: 1

Number of Rooms: 1   Type of Rooms:

Contact Information

Last Name:

First Name:

Street Number:

City:

Province/State:

Country: Canada

Postal Code

Phone Number:

E-mail Address:

Credit Card Information

Credit Card: ○ Visa ○ MasterCard ○ American Express ○ Discover

Name on Credit Card:

Credit Card Number: (No spaces or dashes, please)

Expiration Date: (MM/YYYY)

[Submit]   [Reset]

2.* Draw an ERD that describes GreenHeating database about its heating units, the house in which they locate, and its technicians and the services they perform for the heating units. Each heating unit has a unique unit number, name, manufactory, type, date built, and capacity. House has a unique address, owner, and insurance. A heating unit can be used in one house. A house can have several heating units or it can have no heating unit. A technician has a unique employee number, employee name, title, and year hired. Some technicians supervise others. Every heating unit has been cared for by at least one and generally many technicians; each technician has cared for at least one and generally many heating units. Each time when a technician performs a specific service for a heating unit, the service type, date, and time are recorded.

Minicase: *GreenJetNB (Chapter 3)*

GreenJetNB is a regional airline with headquarters in New Bedford. It has several aircrafts and various commute itineraries between hubs and small cities. GreenJetNB wants to have data on the current aircraft and pilots who works on each of its aircrafts. For scheduling and marketing purposes, it keeps track data of past and future flights and data of the passengers who traveled with GreenJetNB and have booked on the future flights. A flight is identified by a unique flight number. It is described by a departure city, a destination city, a departure time, an arrival time, and a schedule code (i.e., D for daily, M for Monday, MW for Monday and Wednesday, etc.). A flight involves just one aircraft, but an aircraft can serve on many flights. Each aircraft can have more than one pilots and each pilot can drive more than one aircraft. Each aircraft has its attributes include GreenJetNB aircraft number, manufacturing serial number, type, and capacity. GreenJetNB keeps the maintenance records for each aircraft to trace the maintenance work, the time, and the responsible persons. The maintenance work is outsourced to several independent maintenance companies. Each pilot has a unique identification number, name, home address, email, and qualification. Some of the pilots are in supervisory positions for several junior pilots. A passenger is identified by a unique number, name, address, and data of birth. GreenJetNB also wants to keep track of the sale price and regular price for each airticket as well as customer satisfaction rating of the trip.

Draw an ERD that models the data for GreenJetNB.

CHAPTER 4. RELATIONAL DATABASE

4.1. Relational Data Model and Tables

Since the 1980s, the **relational data model** has been popularized. At the present time, relational database systems are still the most commonly used database systems. A relational data model is easy to understand and easy to use. Newly developed data bases are all relational data bases, with few exceptions.

In the relational data model, an **entity** can be represented by a **table** (or **relation**). For instance, STUDENT is an entity. Instances of STUDENT can be represented by a table, say, tblStudent, in the database, as shown in Figure 4.1.

Several special terms used in the relational data model are shown in the figure. Each table can have several columns, called **attributes** (or **fields**). An attribute describes a characteristic of the entity. In this example, the entity STUDENT has four attributes: StudentID, StudentName, StudentAddress, and StudentYear. The table can contain many **rows**, and each row represents a **record** (or a **tuple**). A specific attribute(s) that determines the unique record is called **primary key** (or **key**). In this example, StudentID is the key. The value of the key of a record is fixed for the database and is not supposed to be changed.

Each attribute has its **data type**. For example, StudentName is **text** (or **character**, or **string**), and StudentYear is **Number**. The definitions and names of data types are highly dependent on the DBMS. Commonly used data types in database are:

- Text (Character, String);
- Number;
- Integer;
- Date;
- Image.

It is recommended to use **text** for the data type of keys to differentiate strings from numbers. For example, "001" is a character string, and its value is placed in a pair of quotation marks. In terms of internal code within the computer, "001" is different from 1.

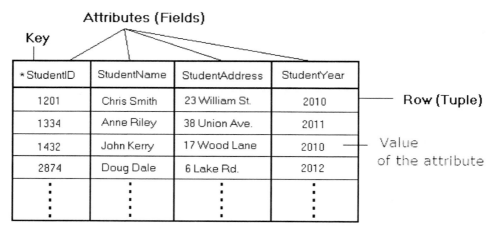

Figure 4.1. Table tblStudent

There are several properties of table in the relational data model.

(1) The order of columns of a relation is not important. In other words, it makes no difference whether you put an attribute, say, StudentID, in the first column or in the second column.

(2) The order of row of a relation is not important. In other words, it makes no difference whether you put a record in the first row or in the second row.

(3) Each **cell** in the table can have only one single value. The value could be "**null**".

(4) No two records in a relation have the same value of primary key.

4.2. Candidate Key and Alternative Key

A relation can have more than one attribute (or a combination of attributes) that can be used to identify the unique record in the table. For instance, if we assume StudentName (including first name, middle name, and last name) is unique in the database, then the STUDENT relation can have two **candidate keys**: StudentID and

StudentName. If the DBA chooses StudentID to be the primary key for the STUDENT relation, then StudentName is called the **alternative key**. If the DBA chooses StudentName to be the primary key for tblStudent, then StudentID becomes the alternative key.

Apparently, the concept of candidate key and alternative key is useful for understanding indexing in databases, as we have discussed in Chapter 2. Now we have four terms about key: primary key, candidate key, alternative key, and foreign key.

4.3. Conversion of ER Model to Relational Data Model

The conversion of an ERD into the relational data model includes two steps: constructing relations, and defining constraints. As you can see in this chapter, it is one seamless step to convert a physical ERD into the relational data model. In fact, the ER model in the physical ERD form (i.e., the form that has 1:1 or 1:M relationship, associative entity, and foreign keys, as presented in Chapter 3) and the relational data model represent the same concept in the alternative forms. In fact, the ER model is the human perception of the database, and the relational data model is the computer internal model of the database.

4.3.1. Constructing relations

The general rules of conversion of the ER model to the relational data model are simple if the physical ERD is used.

(1) An entity (including associative entity) in the ER model is a relation in the relational data model.

(2) All attributes (including intersection data items) in an entity in the ER model are the attributes of the corresponding relation in the relational data model.

(3) The primary key of an entity in the ER model is the primary key of the corresponding relation in the relational data model.

(4) The foreign key in an entity in the ER model is an attribute of the corresponding relation in the relational data model.

Figure 4.2 shows the result of conversion of the ER model in Figure 3.9 to the relational model. The relational data model in Figure 4.3 is the result of conversion of the ER model in Figure 3.13.

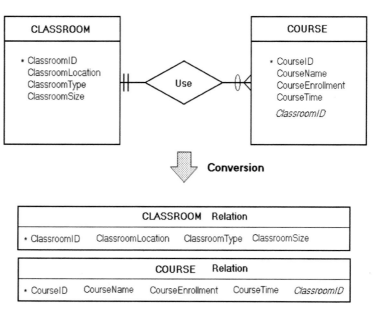

Figure 4.2. ER Model in Figure 3.9 Is Converted to Relational Model

STUDENT	Relation		
* StudentID	StudentName	StudentAddress	StudentYear

PROFESSOR	Relation		
* ProfessorID	ProfessorName	ProfessorTelephone	ProfessorEmail

COURSE	Relation		
* CourseID	CourseName	CourseEnrollment	CourseTime

TEACH	Relation		
* ProfessorID	* CourseID	* StudentID	Assessment

Figure 4.3. The Relational Data Model Converted from the ER Model in Figure 3.13

The relations can be created as tables of the database under the DBMS support. There are two ways to creating tables in DBMS: SQL and/or graphical environment. We will learn SQL in Chapter 6. Technical Guide II in this textbook describes the graphical environment in Microsoft Access for creating tables.

A relation filled with data is a **data sheet**. Figure 4.4 is a sample of data sheet of the STUDENT relation.

STUDENT	Relation		
* StudentID	StudentName	StudentAddress	StudentYear
1201	Chris Smith	23 William St.	2010
1334	Anne Riley	38 Union Ave.	2011
1432	John Kerry	17 Wood Lane	2010
2874	Doug Dale	6 Lake Rd.	2012

Figure 4.4. Sample Data Sheet of the STUDENT Relation

4.3.2. Defining constraints

The second step of conversion of the ER model into the relational data model defines the constraints for cardinalities and modalities attached to the relationships between entities. Generally, a **constraint** is a restriction posted on data to enforce rules. To implement the cardinalities and modalities in the ER model, the database designer must define applicable constraints that are attached to the corresponding tables.

The reality is that the methods of implementation of constraints attached to tables vary depending upon the DBMS, although the methods of construction of tables are quite standard in all relational DBMSs. In this textbook, we use a generic form of script, called **pseudo-code**, to define constraints attached to tables.

(1) For a relationship with 1:M cardinality, no constraint is needed as it is the default case.

(2) For a relationship with 1:1 cardinality, define the constraint using the following pseudo-code:

Table {CONSTRAINT *foreign-key* UNIQUE}

For instance, for the 1:1 relationship between PROFESSOR and OFFICE in Figure 3.8, the constraint is defined as follows.

PROFESSOR {CONSTRAINT *OfficeID* UNIQUE}

(3) For a relation with 1 modality, no constraint is needed as it is the default case. Nevertheless, the following pseudo-code can be used to make the default constraint explicit.

Table {CONSTRAINT MANDATORY TO The-Other-Table}

For instance, in the Figure 3.8 example, the following constraint imposes 1 modality to the OFFICE table which means that there must be at least one instance of OFFICE in the relationship between OFFICE and PROFESSOR.

OFFICE {CONSTRAINT MANDATORY TO PROFESSOR}

(4) For a relation with 0 modality, define the constraint using the following pseudo-code.

Table {CONSTRAINT OPTIONAL TO The-Other-Table}

For instance, in the Figure 3.8 example, the following constraint imposes 0 modality to the PROFESSOR table which means that the minimum instance of PROFESSOR could be 0 in the relationship between PROFESSOR and OFFICE.

PROFESSOR {CONSTRAINT OPTIONAL TO OFFICE}

When implementing the constraints expressed in pseudo-code using a particular

DBMS, the database designer must examine the support features of the DBMS used for the database construction. Sophisticated commercial DBMS support advanced SQL features that allow the database designer to define those constraints using SQL. Technical Guide II in this textbook shows limited features of implementation of constraints in the Microsoft Access environment.

One interesting point is that, unlike entity, a relationship represented by the diamond shape in ERD has no its corresponding representative in the relational database. That is why some versions of ERD notations even do not have diamond shape for relationships. In our physical ERD notations, we keep the diamond shape for two reasons. First, ERD is a tool for representing the semantic network of the database. To describe the database in a genuine semantic context, we need to represent the relationships explicitly on the diagram for human communication about the meaning of the database. Second, as we learned earlier, the nature of associative entities is different from that of ordinary entities, and we need to use the diamond shape to differentiate associative entities from ordinary entities. To make the notations consistent, we must keep the diamond notation clearly in the ERD.

4.4. Data Retrieval from Relational Database

Once the relational data model is established, the DBMS allows the user to create tables, to establish the relationships, and to input data. The tables along with the data become a relational database. Supported by the DBMS, the user is allowed to retrieve data from the relational database through **SQL (Structured Query Language)**, which will be introduced in Chapter 6, or its alternative called **Query By Examples** (**QBE**) technique, as explained in Technical Guide II of this textbook for using QBE in Microsoft Access.

There is **relational algebra** to formally describe how data can be retrieved from a relational database. Intuitively, the way in which data are retrieved from a relational database is the search-and-match among the tables.

4.4.1. B-trees for search-and-match

Once a relational database is built, the DBMS can create B-trees to index the selected attributes for the database to support data search and data direct access. As we learned from Chapter 2, however, excessive B-trees make data retrievals from each of the tables in the relational database efficiently, although they consume computational resource for maintenance.

4.4.2. Simple data retrieval path

In simple data retrieval cases, it is possible to define a clear data retrieval path. For instance, in the relational database represented by the tables in Figure 4.3, to *"find the assessment made by professor Fred Brown for student Chris Smith in the Database Design & Implementation course"*, the database goes through the following steps while each step involves just one table, as illustrated in Figure 4.5.

• Find the primary key of Professor Fred Brown from the PROFESSOR relation;

• Find the primary key of student Chris Smith from the STUDENT relation;

• Find the primary key of course Database Design & Implementation from the COURSE relation;

• Use the three primary keys as the combination key to find the assessment in the TEACH relation.

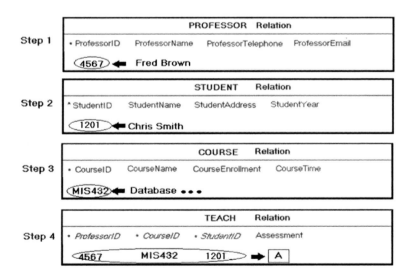

Figure 4.5. Simple Case of Data Retrieval

4.4.3. Join operation

When highly integrated data are retrieved from multiple tables, however, the data retrieval becomes complicated. For instance, in the relational database represented by the tables in Figure 4.2, to "*list course ID, course title, course enrollment, course time for each course along with its classroom's data including classroom ID, classroom type, classroom size*", the database must go back-forth between the two tables (i.e., COURSE and CLASSROOM) for many times, and meanwhile store a large amount of intermediate data before it can present the final query result to the user. In such a case, the database actually performs a **join** operation. The join operation matches the values of the key in one relation (ClassroomID in the CLASSROOM relation) and the values of the foreign key in the other relation (*ClassroomID* in the COURSE relation) to merge the two relations into a single table, as illustrated in Figure 4.6. Note that the merged table (COURSE-CLASSROOM) should have the same number of rows as the relation on the M side (COURSE) of the 1:M relationship.

Apparently, the merged table contains data redundancy, but provides integrated data for the query. Clearly, the join operation would take enormous computation resources if the tables involved are huge. Sophisticated DBMS apply advanced algorithms to optimize join operations.

COURSE-CLASSROOM

CourseID	CourseName	CourseEnrollment	CourseTime	**ClassroomID**	ClassroomLocation	ClassroomType	ClassroomSize
MIS212	Programming	40	MWF 9-10	T-001	T-Building	Comp-Lab	50
MIS432	Database	30	MWF 11-12	T-001	T-Building	Comp-Lab	50
ACT211	Accounting I	40	TR 10-11	L-213	L-Building	Lecture	60
FIN312	Finance	35	MWF 9-10	L-213	L-Buldinbg	Lecture	60
MGT211	Organization	38	TR 10-11	K-123	K-Bulding	Case-Room	40

Figure 4.6. Merge Tables through Join Operation

4.5. Referential Integrity

As the primary key in the table on the 1-side is the foreign key in the table on the M-side in a 1:M relationship, there are potential violations of data integrity. For example, in the relational database represented in Figure 4.2, when the user adds a course to the COURSE table, he might make a mistake that the inputted classroom ID for the course even does not exist. Also, when the user deletes a classroom records but the classroom has already been assigned to several courses, what should the database do? Such problems are known as **referential integrity**.

Any DBMS should be capable to maintain referential integrity and to prevent potential violations of data integrity. When the data are inputted into the database, the DBMS must apply the rule to check the inputted data for referential integrity. For example, the DBMS never allows the user to input a value of ClassroomID (foreign key) in the COURSE table if the value of ClassroomID does not exist in the CLASSROOM table. For data deletion, the referential integrity issue is a little more complicated than data insertion. Generally, there are three **delete rules** as described below.

(1) Delete Rule: Restrict

Suppose one wants to delete a classroom record (on the 1-side), and the classroom has been assigned to courses (on the M-side) already. The restrict rule will forbid the delete to take place. A classroom record is allowed to be deleted only when it has not been assigned to any course.

(2) Delete Rule: Cascade

If the cascade rule is applied, when a record on the 1-side is deleted, all related records on the M-side will be deleted as well. In the Figure 4.2 example, if one deletes a classroom record, all records of the courses which use the classroom will be deleted automatically.

(3) Delete Rule: Set-to-Null

If the set-to-null rule is applied, when a record on the 1-side is deleted, the matching foreign key values on the M-side will be changed to "null". In the Figure 4.2 example, if a classroom record is deleted, all courses that have been assigned to this classroom will be changed to "null" that means "no classroom".

These delete rules are implemented by the DBMS through constraints. Again, the methods of implementing these constraints vary depending upon the DBMS used. Large DBMSs support advanced SQL features that allow the database designer to implement more constraints. Technical Guide II in this textbook shows some features of delete rule constraints in the Microsoft Access environment.

Chapter 4 Exercises

1.* Consider the tables in Figure 4.3. Assume that course names are unique. Mark all primary keys (PK), candidate keys (CK), alternative keys (AK), and foreign keys (FK) on the tables.

2. Convert the following ERD into a relational database model. Explain your assumptions for making candidate keys. Mark all primary keys (PK), candidate keys (CK), alternative keys (AK), and foreign keys (FK) on the tables. Mark the data type (T or N) for each attribute.

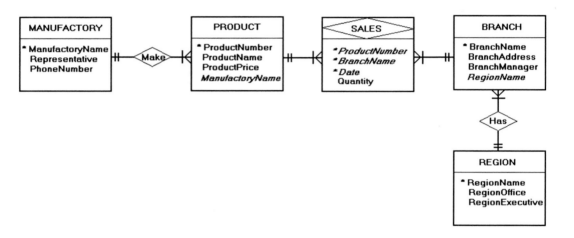

3. Consider the following data sheets of the database represented in Question 1.

MANUFACTORY

* ManufactoryName	Representative	PhoneNumber
RedFlower	John	2345
BlueJay	Anne	3456
GreenWorld	Dick	4567
YellowRock	Mary	7890

PRODUCT

* ProductNumber	ProductName	ProductPrice	*ManufactoryName*
C1234	ThinkPC	2000	GreenWorld
B3456	SmartPhone	3000	BlueJay
A7213	GW-GPS	500	GreenWorld
A8934	YR-GPS	450	YellowRock
C8973	MobilPrinter	480	GreenWorld

SALES

ProductNumber	*BranchName*	*Date	Quantity
C1234	Westport	03/12/2012	123
B3456	Eastport	03/23/2012	234
A7213	Northport	04/02/2012	58
C1234	Southport	03/08/2012	34
A7213	Westport	04/23/2012	134
A8934	Eastport	05/05/2012	88

BRANCH

*BranchName	BranchAddress	BranchManager	RegionName
Eastport	20 Eastport Rd.	Tim	NewBedford
Northport	50 Northport Ave.	Mike	Boston
Southport	60 Southport St.	Susan	FallRiver
Westport	10 Westport Dr.	Cathy	CapeCod

a) Does it cause data redundancy to place ManufactoryName in both MANUFACTORY and PRODUCT tables? Why?

b) Merge the PRODUCT table and SALES table into a single table. Show the products that have sales. Do you see data redundancy in the merged table? Give an example. Does the merged table have any advantage?

4. Consider the relational database represented by the ER diagram in Question 1 and the datasheets in Question 2. Explain how the following data are retrieved from the relational database in step-by-step, be specific by showing the data.

a) Find the record of product number A8934.

b) Find the record of the product of "ThinkPC".

c) List all of the names of representatives of the manufactory companies that produce "ThinkPC".

d) What is the sales figure of "ThinkPC" at Cathy's branch on 03/12/2012?

e) List all product sales transactions for year 2012, including the product numbers, product names, product prices, sales, branches for the sales, and the manufactories for the products.

f) List the branch names, branch manager names, product numbers, product names, and sales quantity for every sales transaction that occurred during year 2012.

5. Consider the following the database represented in Question 1 and the datasheet in Question 2. What would happen in the following situations?

a) The deletion rule between the MANUFACTORY and PRODUCT relations is restrict and an attempt is made to delete the record for ManufactoryName "GreenWorld" in the MANUFACTORY relation.

b) The deletion rule between the MANUFACTORY and PRODUCT relations is restrict and an attempt is made to delete the record for ManufactoryName "RedFlower" in the MANUFACTORY relation.

c) The deletion rule between the MANUFACTORY and PRODUCT relations is restrict and an attempt is made to delete the record for ManufactoryName "BlueJay" in the PRODUCT relation.

d) The deletion rule between the MANUFACTORY and PRODUCT relations is cascade and an attempt is made to delete the record for ManufactoryName "GreenWorld" in the MANUFACTORY relation.

e) The deletion rule between the MANUFACTORY and PRODUCT relations is cascade and an attempt is made to delete the record for ManufactoryName "RedFlower" in the MANUFACTORY relation.

f) The deletion rule between the MANUFACTORY and PRODUCT relations is cascade and an attempt is made to delete the record for ManufactoryName "BlueJay" in the PRODUCT relation.

g) The deletion rule between the MANUFACTORY and PRODUCT relations is set-to-null and an attempt is made to delete the record for ManufactoryName "GreenWorld" in the MANUFACTORY relation.

h) The deletion rule between the MANUFACTORY and PRODUCT relations is set-to-null and an attempt is made to delete the record for ManufactoryName "RedFlower" in the MANUFACTORY relation.

i) The deletion rule between the MANUFACTORY and PRODUCT relations is set-to-null and an attempt is made to delete the record for ManufactoryName "BlueJay" in the PRODUCT relation.

Minicase: *GreenJetNB (Chapter 4)*

Follow the GreenJetNB minicase in Chapter 3, convert the ERD you generated for GreenJetNB into a relational database. Define constraints for each table.

CHAPTER 5. NORMALIZATION AND LOGICAL DATABASE DESIGN

5.1. Normalization

It is possible that the tables created for the relational database have problems of data redundancy, because the ER modeling itself does not ensure no-redundancy. **Normalization** is a process that evaluates the table structures and minimizes data redundancy. Specifically, normalization is an analysis procedure to group attributes into well-structured relations and obtain "good" relations (tables) for the relational database by eliminating the risk of data redundancy.

5.2. Functional Dependency

An important concept of normalization is **functional dependency** which defines the **determination relationships** between the attributes. The concept of functional dependency is not totally new to you. We have introduced the concept of **primary key**. Using the term of functional dependency, we can say "*a record of the table is **functionally dependent** on the primary key of the table*," or "*the primary key of the table is the **determinant** of a record of the table*." In normalization, functional dependency reaches to the attribute level instead of the record level.

Formally, the statement "*B is functionally dependent on A*" or "*A determines B*", where B is an attribute, A is an attribute or a group of attributes, means that "*if you know the value A, then you know the value of B.*" The common notation of functional dependency is

$$A \rightarrow B$$

For example, in the database represented in Figure 4.3, if you know the StudentID, then we can determine the StudentName of this student. Formally,

$$StudentID \rightarrow StudentName$$

If you know the [StudentID+CourseID+ProfessorID], then we can determine the Assessment for this student, this course, and by this professor. Formally,

[StudentID+CourseID+ProfessorID] $\rightarrow$ Assessment

One point we would like to underline here is the conceptualization. The functional dependencies for a database are assumed by the database designer based on her/his conceptual understanding of the relationships between the attributes in the real world. The functional dependencies for the database are usually objective "common sense", but can also be assumptions which may or may not be totally objective. However, if an assumption of functional dependency is contradictory with what really happens in the real world, the database might build in errors. As functional dependency is used as the key instrument for the normalization process, different assumptions of functional dependencies for the database may result in different outcomes of database design. Apparently, the conceptualization of the real world is crucial for the database development. Practically, if you design a database, you need to document the assumptions of functional dependencies beyond "common sense" for the database to avoid confusion. These assumptions become the **business rules** for the database. If you are using a database, you would respect the business rules made for the database, and do not make your own assumptions.

5.3. Normal Forms

A table has its properties in terms of the functional dependencies between its attributes. A **normal form** represents a certain type of functional dependency property of tables. Normal forms are ordered in a series of stages. A table in a higher stage of normal form is better than a table in lower stage of normal form in terms of data redundancy and anomaly control. The normalization process is to evaluate tables and convert tables in a lower stage of normal form into tables in a higher stage of normal form. We will emphasize on **first normal form (1NF)**, **second normal form (2NF)**, and **third normal form (3NF)**, although will also study higher-level normal forms. For most business databases, tables in 3NF are considered to be acceptable with no serious data redundancy.

Note the concepts that (1) if a table in 3NF, it must be also in 2NF; (2) if a table in 2NF, it must be in 1NF as well; (3) the database is in 3NF only if all tables are in 3NF.

5.3.1. Unnormalized form

A table is called unnormalized, or **0NF**, if it has a missing value or multiple values in a cell, or has not primary key. Figure 5.1 shows examples of unnormalized table.

Student ID	Student Name	Course ID	Grade
10001	Chris Smith	ACT211	A
		MIS315	B
		MIS322	
10021	Anne Riley	ACT212	B
		MGT311	
		FIN312	A
10293	John Kerry	MGT212	B
		ACT211	A

(a) Table with missing values or multiple values

Student ID	Student Name	Grade
10001	Chris Simth	A
10001	Chris Simth	B
10001	Chris Simth	B
10021	Anne Riley	B
10021	Anne Riley	A
10021	Anne Riley	A
10293	John Kerry	B
10293	John Kerry	A

(b) Table with no primary key

Figure 5.1. Unnormalized (0NF) Tables

5.3.2. First normal form (1NF)

A table is in **first normal form** (**1NF**) if it meets the following two conditions.

(1) The table has no missing value or multiple values in a cell.

(2) The primary key of the relation is identified based on assumptions of functional dependency among all attributes. These assumptions should be consistent with the

business rules in the business environment.

*StudentID	StudentName	Major	Department	*CourseID	CourseTitle	Grade
10003	John Smith	ACT	Accounting	ACT211	Fin.Accouting	B
10003	John Smith	ACT	Accounting	ENG101	Intro.English I	A
10014	Anne Gold	CHM	Chemistry	CHM101	Intro.Chemistry	C
10014	Anne Gold	CHM	Chemistry	CHM231	Adv.Chemistry	B
12343	Bob Brown	GNS	Biology	BIO101	Intro.Biology	A
12343	Bob Brown	GNS	Biology	CHM101	Intro.Chemistry	B
12343	Bob Brown	GNS	Biology	BIO345	Genetics II	A
13345	Mike Green	ACT	Accounting	ENG101	Intro.English I	B
13345	Mike Green	ACT	Accounting	ENG201	Intro.English II	B
13345	Mike Green	ACT	Accounting	ENG345	Literature	C

Figure 5.2. Table in 1NF

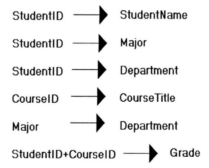

Figure 5.3. Functional Dependency for the 1NF Table in Figure 5.2

Figure 5.2 shows an example of table in 1NF. The assumptions of functional dependency among all attributes are then made, as shown in Figure 5.3. Based on the assumptions of functional dependency, it is conclude that the primary key of this 1NF table is [StudentID+CourseID] (a **combination key**), which is marked with asterisk (*), since [*StudentID+*CourseID] is the determinant of any other attribute in the table. In other words, if you know a value of [*StudentID+*CourseID], you will know all values of other 5 attributes.

5.3.3. Conversion from 0NF to 1NF

The procedure of converting from a 0NF table into 1NF table includes the following steps.

Step 1: Eliminate missing values or repeating values in any cell.

Step 2: Define all functional dependencies among the attributes based on the business environment or common sense. If there is an attribute without involving functional dependency (e.g., Grade in the example in Figure 5.1(b)), you must create a functional dependency for it by adding a new attribute(s) (e.g., in Figure 5.1(b), add CourseID to make [StudentID+CourseID] for Grade in the table).

Step 3: Identify the primary key for the table (e.g., [*StudentID+*CourseID] in Figure 5.2), so that if the value of the primary key is known then the value of any other attribute must be known.

5.3.4. Data modification anomaly

The 1NF table in Figure 5.2 has problems. First, the data are redundant. For instance, the fact that student 10014 is Anne Gold is stored twice. This not only wastes resource, but also causes problems called **data modification anomaly**.

(1) **Update anomaly**

In a table with data redundancy, if a repeated fact is changed, all redundant values must be changed in each place they are stored. This is called update anomaly. For example, in Figure 5.2, if the name of Student with Student ID 10014 is changed to Anne Smith, all records with Student ID 10014 have to be changed correspondingly.

(2) **Insertion anomaly**

A table with data redundancy could preclude useful facts. For example, the table in

Figure 5.2 is unable to record a newly admitted student unless she/he has taken a course because CourseID is a part of the primary key which can't be empty. This problem is called insertion anomaly. The insertion anomaly in a table with data redundancy actually eliminates useful facts.

(3) **Deletion anomaly**

In a table with data redundancy, a deletion of record from the table can cause unintentional deletion of facts. For instance, in Figure 5.2, if Student #10003 John Smith withdraws his ACT211 course and the first record in the table is deleted, then the fact that ACT211 is Fin.Accounting will be unintentionally lost. This problem is known as deletion anomaly.

5.3.5. Second normal form (2NF)

As you can see in Figure 5.2, a great deal of data redundancy is caused by the mixture of student data and course data. The root of this problem is known as **partial key dependency**; that is, student data depend on StudentID only (not [StudentID+CourseID]), and course data depend on CourseID only (not [StudentID+CourseID]).

To eliminate the partial key dependency, the 1NF table is decomposed into two or more tables which do not have partial key dependency. The rule of decomposition is to make such tables that all attributes depend on the entire key.

The form of tables without partial key dependency is called second normal form or 2NF. Figure 5.4 shows the result of decomposition of the 1NF table in Figure 5.2, and the functional dependencies relevant to each table in 2NF.

The key of the STUDENT table is a single attribute, and thus this table can never have partial key dependency. The COURSE table has the same condition. The GRADING table has a combination key, and Grade fully depends on [StudentID+CourseID]. Hence, these three tables are in 2NF. Clearly, these tables are also in 1NF.

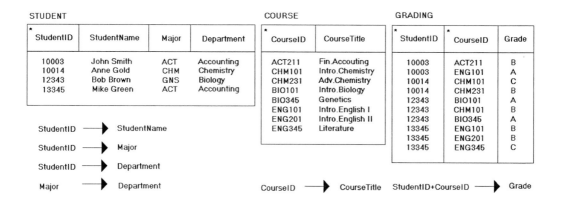

Figure 5.4. Tables in 2NF

As you can see in Figure 5.4, because the partial key dependency has been eliminated, the data redundancy is greatly eliminated as well. Here, we refresh what we have learned from Chapter 1 about data redundancy. In Figure 5.4, StudentID 10003 appears once in the STUDENT table and 2 times in the GRADING table. These values are not data redundancy because they record different facts.

5.3.6. Conversion from 1NF to 2NF

The procedure of converting from a 1NF table into 2NF tables includes the following steps.

Step 1: Make a list of potential individual key components derived from the primary key of the original table in 1NF. Each key component will become the primary key of a new table. For example, for the table in 1NF in Figure 5.2, three potential individual primary keys can be derived from [StudentID+CourseID]; they are:

StudentID
CourseID
[StudentID+CourseID]

Step 2: For each attribute in the table in 1NF, assign it to the pertinent functionally dependent potential individual key. The tables in 2NF are then formed. Using the example of Figure 5.2 and Figure 5.3, you can assign StudentName to StudentID, CourseTitle to CourseID, Grade to [StudentID+CourseID], and so on. The final result of the two steps for the example in Figure 5.2 is shown in Figure 5.4.

A special case is worth noting. If a key component with two or more attributes does not have non-key data, then the database designer must justify assumptions in order to determine whether this key component can become a table with its primary key only. For example, suppose the table in Figure 5.2 does not have attribute Grade. [StudentID+CourseID] could still be meaningful as an independent table without a non-key attribute, indicating *"who had taken what course"*. It is clear that the assumption of business rule made here is: *"any value of the combination [StudentID+CourseID] is unique"*. This assumption is true if *"a student can take a particular course with only one record"*, but it is not true if *"a student can have many records for a particular course"*.

5.3.7. Third normal form (3NF)
A table in 2NF can still contain data redundancy. For instance, the STUDENT table in Figure 5.4 has repeating data of major and department. This problem is caused by **non-key dependency** (or **transitive dependency**); that is, the Major attribute is a non-key attribute, but it is the determinant of the Department attribute. You can do the following steps to solve this problem.
(1) Create a new table (e.g., OWNERSHIP) for the attributes involved in the non-key dependency (e.g., Major and Department);
(2) The primary key for this new table is the determinant involved in the non-key dependency (e.g., Major);
(3) Keep the determinant attribute involved in the non-key dependency (e.g., Major) in the original table (STUDENT in this example) as the foreign key from the new table (e.g., OWNERSHIP), and delete other attributes involved in the non-key dependency (e.g., Department) from the original table (STUDENT in this example).

The form of tables without non-key dependency is called third normal form or

3NF. Figure 5.5 shows the result of decomposition of the 2NF table in Figure 5.4 as well as the functional dependencies relevant to each table. Clearly, the tables in 3NF are also in 2NF.

There is one point to clarify for the definition of non-key dependency in 3NF. If an attribute is an alternative key, it is not considered to be a non-key attribute. For instance, in the STUDENT table in Figure 5.5, if StudentName is unique and is considered to be an alternative key of the table, it is not a non-key attribute. Actually, it does not cause data redundancy.

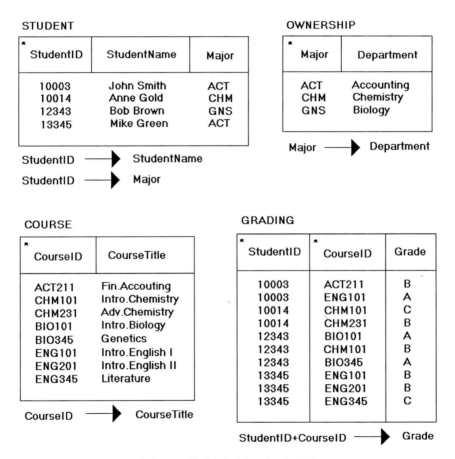

Figure 5.5. Tables in 3NF

5.3.8. Conversion from 2NF to 3NF

The procedure of converting from a 2NF table into 3NF tables includes the following steps.

Step 1: Identify any non-key dependency in the table in 2NF. In the example of Figure 5.4, Major → Department is a non-key dependency.

Step 2: Create a new table (e.g., OWNERSHIP in the Figure 5.5 example) for the attributes involved in the non-key dependency (e.g., Major and Department in this example), and assign the primary key for this new table (e.g., Major in this example).

Step 3: Keep the determinant attribute involved in the non-key dependency (e.g., Major in the Figure 5.5 example) in the original table (STUDENT in this example) as the foreign key from the new table (e.g., OWNERSHIP), and delete other attributes involved in the non-key dependency (Department in this example) from the original table (STUDENT in this example).

5.3.9. Summary of normalization procedure from 0NF to 3NF

3NF tables are generally considered to be acceptable for database design. The overall normalization process from 0NF to 3NF is depicted in Figure 5.6.

The overall normalization procedure from 0NF to 3NF that produces well-structured tables and their ERD is summarized in the following steps.

Step 1. Arrange the data into basic tables known as "unnormalized" tables **(0NF)**;

Step 2. Convert the tables in 0NF into 1NF by establishing primary key;

Step 3. Convert the tables in 1NF into 2NF by eliminating partial key dependency;

Step 4. Convert the tables in 2NF into 3NF by eliminating non-key dependency;

Step 5. Consolidate all tables in 3NF from the current analysis and the previous analysis, if any, and generate or revise the ERD.

Technical Guide I in this textbook provides another example of normalization procedure for database design.

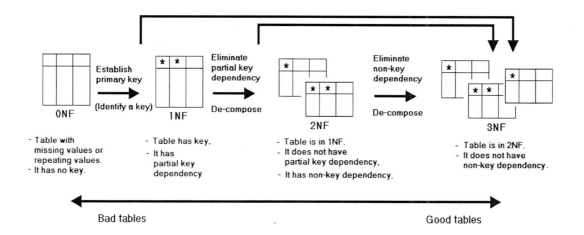

Figure 5.6. Normalization Process

5.3.10. Boyce-Codd Normal Form (BCNF)

Tables in 3NF could still have data redundancy and modification anomalies due to other types of functional dependencies. **BCNF (Boyce-Codd Normal Form)** addresses the problem in a 3NF table where a **non-candidate-key attribute** is the determinant of an attribute of the key of the table. Specifically, BCNF solves two special cases not covered by 3NF: (1) a non-key attribute determines an attribute in a combination key; (2) an attribute in the combination key determines another part of the combination key. In the literature, there is no precise common terminology for such functional dependencies. In this textbook, we call such functional dependencies **"reverse dependency"** because a part of the combination key is reversely determined by another non-candidate-key attribute.

Although the "reverse dependency" problems are not common, they do cause data redundancy. Here we present an example that a table in 3NF is not in BCNF. Suppose there is a table called ADVISING, as shown in Figure 5.7. The functional dependencies based on the business rules indicate that [StudentID+Major] is the combination key of the table, Advisor is dependent on [StudentID+Major], and MajorProject is dependent on [StudentID+Major] as well. There is no dependency between Advisor and MajorProject. Thus, the ADVISING table is in 3NF. However, Advisor is not a candidate key of the table, but is the determinant of Major in this business environment. This causes anomalies. For instance, if the major ACT replaces the advisor, the changes must be made in two or more rows. To solve the problem, decompose and restructure the table into two tables in BCNF, as shown in Figure 5.8.

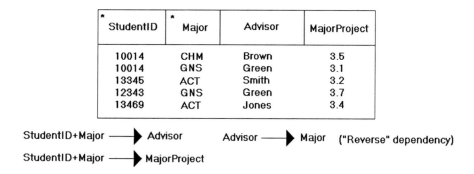

Figure 5.7. A Table in 3NF but Not in BCNF

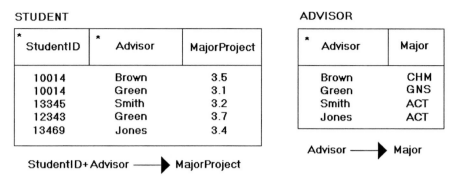

Figure 5.8. Tables in BCNF without "Reverse" Dependency

5.3.11. Conversion from 3NF to BCNF

The procedure of converting from a 3NF table into BCNF tables includes the following steps.

Step 1: Identify any reverse dependency in the table in 3NF. In the example of Figure 5.7, Advisor → Major is a reverse dependency.

Step 2: Create a new table (e.g., ADVISOR in the Figure 5.8 example) for the attributes involved in the reverse dependency (Advisor and Major in this example), and assign the primary key for this new table (Advisor in this example).

Step 3: Make the determinant attribute involved in the reverse dependency (Advisor in the Figure 5.8 example) to be a part of the combination primary key of the original table (STUDENT in this example), and delete other attributes involved in the reverse dependency (Major in this example) from the original table (STUDENT in this example).

Note that the determinant attribute involved in the reverse dependency (Advisor in the Figure 5.8 example) also becomes a foreign key from the new table (e.g.

ADVISOR in the Figure 5.8 example) to the original table (STUDENT in this example).

5.3.12. Fourth normal form (4NF)

4NF addresses multivalued dependency problem. For instance, the STUDENT table in Figure 5.5 is in 3NF, but it can have data redundancy and modification anomalies if a student can have multiple majors (e.g., a student can have both majors in ACT and FIN) because the STUDENT table might repeat the same facts. Using the functional dependency notations, the multivalued dependency is

StudentID $\rightarrow\rightarrow$ Major

Figure 5.9 shows that the multivalued dependency causes repeating student names.

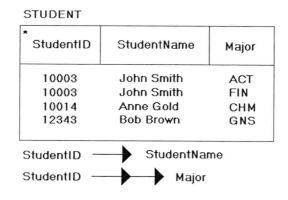

Figure 5.9. Table in 3NF but Not in 4NF

To eliminate the anomalies caused multivalued dependency, the STUDENT table must be decomposed into two tables: the STUDENT table without the Major attribute, and a new table, say, MAJORS which contains the StudentID and Major attributes as the combination key of the table. These two tables are in 4NF, as shown in Figure 5.10.

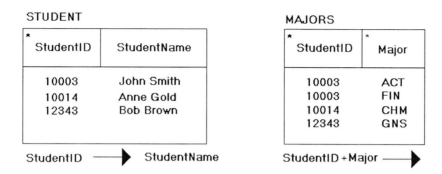

Figure 5.10. Tables in 4NF without Multivalued Dependency

5.3.13. Conversion from 3NF to 4NF

The procedure of converting from a 3NF table into 4NF tables includes the following steps.

Step 1: Identify any multivalued dependency in the table in 3NF. In the example of Figure 5.9, StudentID $\rightarrow\rightarrow$ Major is a multivalued dependency.

Step 2: Create a new table (e.g., MAJORS in the Figure 5.10 example) for the attributes involved in the multivalued dependency (StudentID and Major in this example), and assign the combination primary key for this new table ([StudentID+Major] in this example).

Step 3: Delete the multivalued attribute involved in the multivalued dependency (Major in this example) from the original table (STUDENT in this example).

Note that the primary key attribute in the original table (StudentID in the Figure 5.10 example) also has its corresponding foreign key in the new table (e.g., MAJORS in this example).

5.4. The Nature of Normalization and Higher-Level Normal Forms: 5NF, and DKNF

If you consider Figure 5.8 and Figure 5.10 at once and try to consolidate all attributes StudentID, StudentName, Advisor, Major, MajorProject, etc. for the database in a complicated business environment, you may conclude that once tables are normalized into BCNF and 4NF, the data redundancy is eliminated completely, but, at the same time, the number of tables expands and the data become less integrated. Consequently, normalization purity is often difficult to sustain in large databases because data processing can be prohibitively slow. Nevertheless, many database design experts argue that database tables should be in both BCNF and 4NF.

Our position is clear that the normalization process must be consistent with the clearly defined business rules (functional dependencies) for the database being designed. In principle, a large database for commercial use should be in BCNF and 4NF. However, the decision on the normal form for each table should take the pertinent business rules of the business environment into account. The example of normalization in Technical Guide I in this textbook explains this fine point further.

In fact, even higher-level normal forms such as 5NF and DKNF (Domain Key Normal Form) exist. However, these normal forms mainly fit theoretical purposes such as information science research, but are not practically useful for the databases in the business environment.

5.5. Logical Database Design

Logical database design is the process that defines the databases structures to meet the data requirements of the business. Generally, logical database design includes the following steps.

Step 1. Generate an initial (or trial) ER model for the database through interviews, surveys, observations, and data samples based on the business requirements.

Step 2. Convert the trial ER model into a preliminary set of tables.

Step 3. Perform normalization on the preliminary set of tables into normalized tables (see the procedure in the previous section) based on the assumptions of functional dependencies for the business environment. Determine the final normalized tables, incorporating the consideration of the level of normal forms (3NF, BCNF, or 4NF) for the business environment.

Step 4. Based on the normalized tables, revised the initial ERD to obtain the approved ERD for the database.

Step 5. Convert the normalized tables into the DBMS internal model in the selected DBMS (e.g., Oracle, DB2, Microsoft Access, etc.).

Step 6. Attach pertinent constraints to applicable tables.

Step 7. Verify that the internal model for the selected DBMS is consistent with the approved ER model.

The steps of logical database design are depicted in Figure 5.11. Three points are important to learn.

(1) The logical database design for a database is an iterative process. It refines the ER model and a set of tables for the database through the analysis of business requirements and the normalization process. If the logical design process starts with data samples, Step 1 might be skipped and a preliminary set of tables could be derived directly from the data samples without a trial ERD, as explained by the example in Technical Guide I in this textbook. However, having a trial ERD before the normalization process would make the logical database design less problematic for a large database.

(2) The ERD of a database is a blueprint for the database. It is used for human communication among database designers, DBA, and users to understand the structure of the database. More importantly, because it is difficult for human to verify whether the computer internal model is consistent with those normalized tables without a blueprint, the ERD must be used. Most CASE (Computer Aided Software

Engineering) tools can support mapping from an ERD onto a computer internal model to some extent. As shown in Technical Guide II in this textbook, some DBMS, such as Microsoft Access, can show its computer internal model of those normalized tables in a form of relationships which allows the DBA to verify against the approved ERD.

(3) Logical database design ensures the data needs for the business, but does not take the performance of database into account. As data are normalized into 3NF, or even BCNF and 4NF, the data in tables become more and more detached from each other, and become less and less integrated for the user. The ultimate consequence of data in higher-level normal forms is the inefficiency of data retrieval. To solve this problem in a large database, physical database design must be applied, as discussed in Chapter 7.

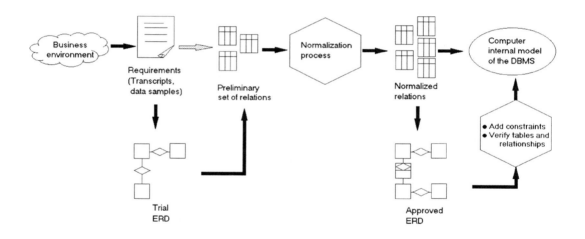

Figure 5.11. Logical Database Design

Chapter 5 Exercises

1. Given the following table, define commonsensical functional dependencies between the attributes.

GreenPlant Auction House Disclosure

Auction Date	Auction Sponsor	Contact	VIN	Make	Model	Year	Miles	Price	Buyer	Buyer Address	Down Payment	Loan Number
09/04/10	N.B.City	j@nbcity.com	AQ122	Ford	Mustang	2010	43k	$25000	Brown	Westport	$500	A-321
09/04/10	N.B.City	j@nbcity.com	B2344	Toyota	Corolla	2009	12k	$13000	Smith	Northport	$280	B-432
09/04/10	RedBank	r@redbank.com	D34R2	Ford	F-250	2011	50k	$35000	Sousa	Eastport	$1000	B-456
09/12/10	RedBank	r@redbank.com	AT343	GMC	Sierra	2010	23k	$34000	Jones	Southport	$750	C-489
09/12/10	YellowBank	s@ybank.com	F45E3	Honda	Accord	2009	19k	$27700	Smith	Northport	$345	A-380
09/23/10	YellowBank	s@ybank.com	P36Y8	Ford	Focus	2009	23k	$10999	Lee	Newport	$210	B-541
09/23/10	BlueCar	t@bluecar.org	K39L9	Toyota	Camry	2010	68k	$29950	Shaw	Oldport	$450	C-543
09/23/10	BlueCar	t@bluecar.org	N2345	Volvo	C90	2010	71k	$32000	O'Neil	Greenport	$621	C-567

2. Given the table in Question 1, provide examples of data insertion anomaly, data deletion anomaly, and data update anomaly.

3.* GreenBook library maintains data on the books. Some of the attributes and functional dependencies are described as follows:

<u>Attributes</u>
BookNumber
PublishDate
BookTitle
FirstAuthor
Length (in pages)
ClientNumber
ClientName
ClientAddress
RentalDate
ReturnDate
RentalFee

<u>Functional Dependencies</u>
BookNumber → BookTitle

BookNumber → FirstAuthor

BookNumber → PublishDate

BookTitle → FirstAuthor

BookTitle → Length

ClientNumber → ClientName

ClientNumber → ClientAddress

[BookNumber+ClientNumber+RentalDate]→
                ReturnDate, RentalFee

For each of the following tables, first write the table's current normal form (as 1NF,

2NF, or 3NF), and explain why. Then, for those tables that are currently in 1NF or 2NF, reconstruct them to be 3NF tables. Primary key attributes are marked with *. Do not assume any functional dependencies other than those shown.

a. *BookTitle, FirstAuthor, Length

b. *BookNumber, PublishDate, BookTitle, FirstAuthor

c. [*BookNumber+*ClientNumber+*RentalDate], ReturnDate, RentalFee

d. [*BookNumber+*ClientNumber+*RentalDate], ClientName,
        ReturnDate, RentalFee

e. [*BookTitle+*ClientNumber], FirstAuthor, Length, ClientName, ClientAddress

4.* GreenSales keeps track of data about products, orders, customers. Each order can include many product items ordered by the same customer. Each ordered product item is specified by sale price and order quantity. The attributes and functional dependencies at GreenSales are assumed as follows. Do not assume any functional dependencies other than those shown.

Attributes	Functional Dependencies
ProductID	ProductID → ProductName
ProductName	CustomerID → CustomerName
CustomerID	CustomerID → CustomerAddress
CustomerName	OrderID → CustomerID
CustomerAddress	OrderID → OrderDate
OrderID	OrderID → ShippingDate
OrderDate	[OrderID+ProductID] → ProductSalePrice
ShippingDate	[OrderID+ProductID] → OrderQuantity
ProductSalePrice	
OrderQuantity	

For each of the following independent tables (primary key attributes are marked with "*", and combination primary key is connected with "+"), explain the table's current normal form (as 1NF, 2NF, or 3NF, and why). Then, for the tables that are currently in 1NF or 2NF, decompose them into 3NF tables, and mark the primary key with "*" for the 3NF tables.

a) *OrderID, OrderDate, ShippingDate, CustomerID, CustomerName, CustomerAddress

b) [*OrderID+*ProductID+*CustomerID], CustomerAddress, ProductName, ProductSalePrice, OrderQuantity

5. GreenPlace is an apartment rental business. It wants to keep track of data of apartment units, parking units, clients, superintendents, and leases. Explain why the following assumptions of functional dependencies of the apartment management system are commonsensical.

ApartmentUnitID → ParkingUnitID
ApartmentUnitID → ApartmentAddress
ApartmentUnitID → ApartmentType
ApartmentUnitID → MonthRental
ApartmentUnitID → Superintendent
ParkingUnitID → ParkingMonthlyFee
ClientID → ClientName
ClientID → → ClientEmployer
[ApartmentUnitID+ClientID] → LeaseStartDate
[ApartmentUnitID+ClientID] → LeaseEndDate

Given the above functional dependencies, for each of the following tables,

(1) explain why the attribute or a combination of attributes marked with * is the primary key of the table;

(2) tell the current normal form (1NF, 2NF, 3NF, BCNF, or 4NF), and explain why;

(3) if the table is not in 3NF, normalize it into tables in 3NF;

(4) if the current table is in 3NF, explain whether the table is in BCNF or 4NF.

Note that, do not make your own assumptions of functional dependency. Each question is independent.

a) *ApartmentUnitID, ApartmentAddress, ApartmentType, Superintendent

b) [*ParkingUnitID+*ClientID], ClientName, ParkingMonthlyFee

c) *ApartmentUnitID, MonthlyRental, ParkingUnitID, ParkingMonthlyFee

d) [*ApartmentUnitID+*ClientID], ClientName, Superintendent,
    MonthlyRental, LeaseEndDate

e) [*ApartmentUnitID+*ClientID+*ParkingUnitID], MonthlyRental,
    ParkingMonthlyFee

f) [*ApartmentUnitID+*ClientID], ClientName, ClientEmployer,
    LeaseStartDate, LeaseEndDate

Minicase: *GreenJetNB (Chapter 5)*

Follow the GreenJetNB minicase in Chapter 3 and Chapter 4. Perform normalization for the tables you generated for the database, and/or justify why the tables are normalized. Re-define or verify the constraints for each normalized table.

CHAPTER 6. DATABASE PROCESSING AND SQL

6.1. Introduction to SQL

SQL (Structured Query Language) is a universal language for creating, updating and querying databases. As SQL is a small language, SQL program is often called SQL script. SQL can be used for all database management systems (DB2, Access, Oracle, etc.) as well as computer language platforms (Java, VB.NET, etc.). SQL was developed under the name SEQUEL by IBM in the mid-1970s. That is why people pronounce SQL as "sequel" more often than "ess-que-ell". SQL has been standardized by ANSI (American National Standard Institute).

When using a particular database management system, we can use the query development environment (i.e. QBE (Query By Examples)) to create queries without using SQL. In those query development environments of QBE, the database management system generates the query code in SQL. In principle, we might not need to write SQL code if we use QBE. However, there are two major reasons for learning SQL.

(1) SQL integrates features of data definition languages (DDL) and data manipulation languages (DML). QBE itself does not possess any features of DDL, such as CREATE and DELETE tables. Also, QBE is unable to implement sophisticated features of DML such as built-in functions in a simple way.

(2) When using large computer languages (such as COBOL, C++, Java, .NET) to develop business application software that is connected to databases (Oracle, DB2, etc.), one must write SQL code that is embedded into the programs in those large computer languages to querying and updating the databases.

The syntax of SQL is quite simple. An SQL script contains a command along with needed clauses, and ends with a semicolon. This section explains how SQL scripts can be used to define and create tables, to insert and update instances of records, retrieve data, and manipulate the data. Suppose we have the design of a tiny database with 3NF tables as shown in Figure 6.1.

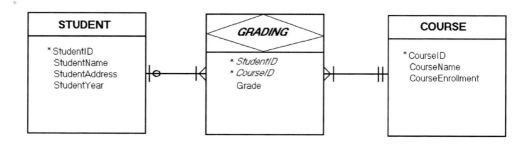

Figure 6.1. The 3NF Tables for SQL Examples in This Chapter

6.2. CREATE and DROP

CREATE TABLE is used to create a table with all attributes and their **data types**. For example, the SQL script in Listing 6.1 creates a table named tblStudent with its four attributes.

```
CREATE TABLE tblStudent
(StudentID CHAR(8),
 StudentName CHAR(20),
 StudentAddress CHAR(20),
 StudentEnrolYear INT,
 PRIMARY KEY (StudentID));
```

Listing 6.1. CREATE TABLE

Common data types used in the standard SQL are:
- CHAR(n) – Character string (text), at most n characters long;
- DATE – Date data;
- DECIMAL(p, q) – Decimal number p digits long and q digits after the decimal point;
- INT – Integer.

You need to use the PRIMARY KEY clause to define the **primary key** of the table. A **combination primary key** could have more than one attribute, e.g.,

```
PRIMARY KEY (StudentID, CourseID)
```

for a two-attribute combination key.

DROP TABLE is used to delete a table. The SQL script in Listing 6.2 deletes tblStudent.

```
DROP TABLE tblStudent;
```

Listing 6.2. DROP TABLE

6.3. INSERT, UPDATE, DELETE

INSERT is used to add one record to the table. The SQL script in Listing 6.3 appends one student record to tblStudent.

```
INSERT INTO tblStudent
VALUES ('01234567', 'John', '285 Westport', 2012);
```

Listing 6.3. INSERT a Record

UPDATE is used to change the value(s) of the record with a certain key value. The SQL script in Listing 6.4 changes the address of the student record with key '01234567'.

```
UPDATE tblStudent
SET StudentAddress = '300 Eastport'
WHERE StudentID='01234567';
```

Listing 6.4. UPDATE a Record

DELETE is used to delete a record with a certain key value. The SQL script in Listing 6.5 deletes the student record with key '01234567'.

```
DELETE FROM tblStudent
WHERE StudentID='01234567';
```

Listing 6.5. DELETE a Record

In the above two examples, condition of the query is defined in the WHERE clause. We will discuss the WHERE clause in more detail later in a special section.

The above SQL commands we have learned are used for database construction and maintenance. These SQL commands fit in the category of database DDL. The SQL scripts with these commands can be embedded in the large computer programs to allow the user to update the database. Apparently, it is not convenient to use these SQL commands to build a database from scratch. Practically, a DBMS can have a user-friendly interface that allows the database designer to create tables and to maintain the tables without using tedious SQL scripts. Microsoft Access is a good example of this, as illustrated in Technical Guide II in this textbook.

Suppose we use the above SQL commands to create the database as modeled in Figure 6.1 that contains the three tables and their instances, as shown in Figure 6.2. We use these data for demonstrating the rest examples of SQL scripts that fit in the category of DML or query.

StudentID	StudentName	StudentAddress	StudentEnrolYear
01234567	John	285 Westport	2012
02345678	Anne	287 Eastport	2014
03456789	Robert	324 Northport	2013

CourseID	CourseName	CourseEnroll
ACT211	Financial Accounting	35
ACT212	Cost Accounting	28
MIS315	Information Systems	40
MIS322	Systems Analysis & Design	38
MIS432	Database Design	30
MKT311	Principles of Marketing	25
MGT490	Special Topics	20

StudentID	CourseID	Grade
01234567	ACT211	A+
01234567	ACT212	A
01234567	MIS315	B
02345678	ACT211	B+
02345678	MIS322	C
03456789	ACT212	B
03456789	MIS432	A
03456789	MKT311	A

Figure 6.2. Sample Database

6.4. Query - SELECT

A **query** is a piece of script that commands the DBMS to retrieve needed data from the database. Queries can generate integrated data from the normalized tables.

In SQL, SELECT command is used to implement queries. The general structure of SELECT query is

```
SELECT      [attributes] [built-in functions]
FROM        [tables]
WHERE       [conditions]
AND         [conditions];
```

Listing 6.6 is an example of a simple query that *"finds the student's name and address of student ID 01234567 from the student table."*

```
SELECT StudentName, StudentAddress
FROM    tblStudent
WHERE StudentID = '01234567';
```

StudentName	StudentAddress
John	285 Westport

Listing 6.6. SELECT to Select Specified Data from a Table

Listing 6.7 is a query that *"finds the student's entire record of student ID 01234567 from the student table."* The "*" sign represents all attributes of the table.

```
SELECT *
FROM tblStudent
WHERE StudentID = '01234567';
```

StudentID	StudentName	StudentAddress	StudentEnrolYear
01234567	John	285 Westport	2012

Listing 6.7. SELECT to Select an Entire Record from a Table

The WHERE clause is used to define conditions. If it is omitted, the query is to retrieve the entire table.

In some cases, the result of a query may contain duplicated data items. To screen out duplicated data items, DISTINCT is used. Consider query: *"Find distinctive student enrollment years from the student table."*

100

```
SELECT DISTINCT StudentEnrolYear
FROM tblStudent;
```

StudentEnrolYear
2012
2013
2014

Listing 6.8. DISTINCT to Eliminate Duplications

6.5. WHERE Clause and Comparison

As shown in the above examples, the WHERE clause defines the conditions for data selection. For comparison, in addition to "=" (equal), comparison operations ">" (greater than), "<" (less than), ">=" (greater than or equal to), "<=" (less than or equal to), and "<>" (not equal to) can be applied in the WHERE clause. Listing 6.9 is query that *"lists the names of those students who enroll to the program after 2011."*


```
SELECT StudentName
FROM tblStudent
WHERE StudentEnrolYear > 2011;
```

StudentName
John
Anne
Robert

Listing 6.9. Comparison - Greater Than

A WHERE clause can have a combination of multiple conditions connected through the **Boolean operators** AND and OR. If the AND operator is applied, the two conditions must be true in order for the combination condition to be true. If the OR operator is applied, at least one of the two conditions must be true in order for the combination condition to be true. When ANDs and ORs are used in the same WHERE clause, ANDs are considered before ORs are considered. To avoid mistakes, it is recommended to use pairs of parenthesis to indicate the consideration priorities. Listing 6.10 is query that *"lists the names of those students whose ID numbers are greater than*

00234567 and who enroll to the program after 2011 or before 2005."

```
SELECT StudentName
FROM tblStudent
WHERE StudentID > '00234567'
AND (StudentEnrolYear > 2011 OR
     StudentEnrolYear < 2005);
```

StudentName
John
Anne
Robert

Listing 6.10. AND and OR Operators

Character strings can also be compared using unequal signs because they are represented by internal code (e.g., ASCII code).

For strings of characters (text), the LIKE operator and a "wildcard" are used to test for a pattern match. Listing 6.11 is a query that *"finds the student records for those students whose street names contain 'Westport'."* Here, the percent sign "%" is a wildcard to represent any collection of characters. Note that, Microsoft Access uses "*" for this type of wildcard.

```
SELECT *
FROM tblStudent
WHERE StudentAddress LIKE '%Westport%';
```

StudentID	StudentName	StudentAddress	StudentEnrolYear
01234567	John	285 Westport	2012

Listing 6.11. LIKE Operator and Wildcard "%"

Listing 6.12 is a query that *"finds the student record for each student whose name has the letter 'o' as the second letter of the name."* Here, the wildcard sign "_" represents any one character. Note that, Microsoft Access uses "?" for this type of wildcard.

```
SELECT *
FROM tblStudent
WHERE StudentName LIKE '_o%';
```

StudentID	StudentName	StudentAddress	StudentEnrolYear
01234567	John	285 Westport	2012
03456789	Robert	324 Northport	2013

Listing 6.12. LIKE Operator and Wildcard "_"

The IN operator allows you to specify a list of character strings to be included in a search. Listing 6.13 is a query that "*finds the student whose ID is '01234567', '00234567', or '00034567'*."


```
SELECT StudentName
FROM tblStudent
WHERE StudentID IN ('01234567',
       '00234567', '00034567');
```

StudentName
John

Listing 6.13. IN Operator

6.6. User Input Request

SQL is mainly embedded into large **host computer programming languages** (e.g., C++, COBOL, Java, .NET, etc.) for database processing on servers. Database manipulation is performed through interactions between SQL and the host language. Direct **SQL-user interaction** is not a main concern of SQL. Nevertheless, many versions of SQL (especially PC versions of SQL) provide means for the user to interact with SQL directly. The user is allowed to input a value directly through SQL that is used to complete the condition in the WHERE clause. For example, one might want to search student based on the user's input of student ID which is not determined by the query itself. In Microsoft Access, this can be done by including user input request, such as:

```
SELECT StudentName
FROM tblStudent
WHERE StudentID=[Please input student ID:];
```

User input request features are commonly available in SQL for the PC environment, and the syntaxes are vary depending on the versions.

6.7. ORDER BY Clause

The ORDER BY clause is used to list data in a particular order based on values of an attribute. The default order is ascending. The ASC operator makes ascending explicit. The DESC operator is used to sort data in the descending order. Listing 6.14 is a query that *"lists all student records in the reverse alphabetic order by student name."*

```
SELECT *
FROM tblStudent
ORDER BY StudentName DESC;
```

StudentID	StudentName	StudentAddress	StudentEnrolYear
03456789	Robert	324 Northport	2013
01234567	John	285 Westport	2012
02345678	Anne	287 Eastport	2014

Listing 6.14. ORDER BY Clause

6.8. Aggregate Functions

Database stores raw data, not secondary (or processed) data such as average, total, etc. to avoid data redundancy. One of the important roles of queries is to provide secondary data as information for the user. SQL uses **aggregate functions** to calculate sums (SUM), averages (AVG), counts (COUNT), maximum values (MAX), and minimum values (MIN). Listing 6.15(a) is a query that "*finds the total number of student records in the student table.*"

```
SELECT COUNT(*)
FROM tblStudent;
```

Listing 6.15(a). COUNT Function

In the query result in Listing 6.15(a), a default name assigned by the DMBS (Expr1000 in Microsoft Access) is used for the query result of aggregation function. If you want to name the result, e.g., CountOfStudents, you use AS keyword, as shown in Listing 6.15(b).

```
SELECT COUNT(*) AS CountOfStudents
FROM tblStudent;
```

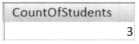

Listing 6.15(b). Use AS Keyword to Define Result Name

Listing 6.16 answers the query "*what are the smallest enrollment number, largest enrollment number, total enrollment number, and average enrollment number in the course table?*"

```
SELECT MIN(CourseEnrollment), MAX(CourseEnrollment),
       SUM(CourseEnrollment), AVG(CourseEnrollment)
FROM tblCourse;
```

Expr1000	Expr1001	Expr1002	Expr1003
20	40	216	30.8571428571429

Listing 6.16. MIN, MAX, SUM, and AVG Functions

Note that, aggregate functions is not allowed to be used in WHERE clause directly. For instance, a clause such like WHERE COUNT(*)>1000 is not allowed.

6.9. GROUP BY Clause and HAVING Clause

When an aggregate function is used, one might want to find the calculated value for **each** group. GROUP BY clause is used to calculate results based on each group. If a condition on the calculated results is needed, the HAVING clause can be added. Listing 6.17 is a query to *"find the total number of courses taken by **each** student, and only include students who have taken at least 2 courses."* Two points are worth noting in this query. First, the query with the GROUP BY clause matches "each" in English. Second, the HAVING clause is different from the condition in the WHERE clause in that the HAVING clause goes with the GROUP BY clause and must use an aggregate function.

```
SELECT StudentID, COUNT(*)
FROM tblGrading
GROUP BY StudentID
HAVING COUNT(*) > 1;
```

StudentID	Expr1001
01234567	3
02345678	2
03456789	3

Listing 6.17. GROUP BY Clause and HAVING Clause

It is possible to add a WHERE clause before GROUP BY. The SQL standard specifies that when WHERE and GROUP BY occur together, the WHERE condition will be applied first. Listing 6.18 is a query to "*find the total number of courses taken by* **each** *student, and only include students whose ID are greater than '01234600' and have taken at least 2 courses.*"

```
SELECT StudentID, COUNT(*)
FROM tblGrading
WHERE StudentID>'01234600'
GROUP BY StudentID
HAVING COUNT(*)>1;
```

StudentID	Expr1001
02345678	2
03456789	3

Listing 6.18. Apply WHERE Clause before GROUP BY Clause

6.10. Joining Tables

Up to this point, all of the queries we have examined deal with a single table. If two or more tables are involved in a query, the **join** operation must be applied. Suppose we are going to "*list the names of those students who receive "A" or "A+" in any course.*" Apparently, two tables, namely, tblStudent and tblGrading, are involved. To join the two tables, the query processor must do the following steps.

(1) Find the value of StudentID in tblGrading for those students who receive "A" or "A+";
(2) Match the values of those StudentID in tblGrading and the StudentID in tblStudent for those students;
(3) Find the StudentName in tblStudent for those students.

Listing 6.19 shows the query.

```
SELECT DISTINCT tblStudent.StudentName
FROM tblGrading, tblStudent
WHERE tblStudent.StudentID=tblGrading.StudentID
AND (tblGrading.Grade='A+' OR
     tblGrading.Grade='A');
```

StudentName
John
Robert

Listing 6.19. Join Two Tables

The SQL script in Listing 6.20 joins the three normalized tables, tblStudent, tblCourse, and tblGrading to integrate all related data in a denormalized form for the user to view.

```
SELECT   *
FROM tblStudent, tblCourse, tblGrading
WHERE tblStudent.StudentID = tblGrading.StudentID
AND tblCourse.CourseID = tblGrading.CourseID;
```

tblStudent.St	StudentNar	StudentAddre	StudentEnr	tblCourse.C	CourseName	CourseEnr	tblGrading.	tblGrading	Grade
01234567	John	285 Westport	2012	ACT211	Financial Accou		35	01234567	ACT211	A+
01234567	John	285 Westport	2012	MIS315	Information Sys		40	01234567	MIS315	B
02345678	Anne	287 Eastport	2014	ACT211	Financial Accou		35	02345678	ACT211	B+
02345678	Anne	287 Eastport	2014	MIS322	Systems Analysi		38	02345678	MIS322	C
03456789	Robert	324 Northport	2013	MIS432	Database Desig		30	03456789	MIS432	A
03456789	Robert	324 Northport	2013	ACT212	Cost Accounting		28	03456789	ACT212	B
03456789	Robert	324 Northport	2013	MKT311	Principles of Ma		25	03456789	MKT311	A
01234567	John	285 Westport	2012	ACT212	Cost Accounting		28	01234567	ACT212	A

Listing 6.20. Join Multiple Tables to Integrate Related Data

In the above example, tables are joined by using the WHERE clause with

conditions. Three general rules are applied in a query with joining tables.
(1) A condition associates two tables, and the general format is:

$$[TableOn\text{-}1\text{-}Side].[PrimaryKey] = [TableOn\text{-}M\text{-}Side].[ForeignKey]$$

(2) If *n* tables are joined in the query, then *n*-1 conditions are needed and are tied by the AND operator.

(3) To differentiate the same names in different tables, the table name followed by a period sign is used for an attribute name (e.g., tblStudent.StudentID) to **qualify** the attribute name. That is, the table name must be quoted as **qualifier** to specify what table the attribute belongs to if the query involves multiple tables.

Listing 6.21 shows another example of query with multiple tables: "*Who (student ID and name) receives "A+" or "A" grade in which course (course ID and course name)? List the results in order of student ID.*"

```
SELECT tblGrading.StudentID, tblStudent.StudentName,
       tblGrading.CourseID, tblCourse.CourseName,
       tblGrading.Grade
FROM tblGrading, tblStudent, tblCourse
WHERE tblStudent.StudentID=tblGrading.StudentID
AND tblCourse.CourseID=tblGrading.CourseID
AND (tblGrading.Grade='A+' OR tblGrading.Grade='A')
ORDER BY tblStudent.StudentID;
```

StudentID	StudentName	CourseID	CourseName	Grade
01234567	John	ACT212	Cost Accounting	A
01234567	John	ACT211	Financial Accounting	A+
03456789	Robert	MKT311	Principles of Marketing	A
03456789	Robert	MIS432	Database Design	A

Listing 6.21. Query with Multiple Tables

6.11. Alternative Format of Inner Join and Outer Join

6.11.1. Explicit inner join clause

The join approach discussed in the previous section is called **inner join** which lists only those rows that satisfy the conditions in the WHERE clause. SQL-92 (SQL Standard 1992) provides an alternative format of inner join as shown in the example of Listing 6.22.

```
SELECT DISTINCT tblStudent.StudentName
FROM tblStudent
INNER JOIN tblGrading
ON tblStudent.StudentID=tblGrading.StudentID
WHERE (tblGrading.Grade='A+' OR
       tblGrading.Grade='A');
```

StudentName
John
Robert

Listing 6.22. Explicit Format of Inner Join

In this format, the FROM clause includes the first table, the INNER JOIN clause includes the second table, and then ON clause specifies the join condition. Apparently, this format could be confusing if three or more tables are involved, and thus is not recommended for the SQL beginners.

6.11.2. Outer join

Outer join is to list all the rows from one of the tables in a join, regardless of whether or not they match any rows in a second table. There are three types of outer join: **left outer join** (all rows from the first table are included, but only the matched rows from the second table are included), **right outer join** (only the matched rows

110

from the first table are included, but all rows from the second table are included), and **full outer join** (all rows from both tables are included). Practically, outer join is not used often. Listing 6.23 shows an example of left outer join that is to "*list the course ID and course name for all grades. Include all courses in the results. For courses that do not have grade records, omit the grade.*" The execution result of this example of left outer join shows that the course MGT490 without matching grades is also included.

```
SELECT tblCourse.CourseID, tblCourse.CourseName,
       tblGrading.Grade
FROM tblCourse LEFT JOIN tblGrading
     ON tblCourse.CourseID=tblGrading.CourseID;
```

CourseID	CourseName	Grade
MIS315	Information Systems	B
MIS322	Systems Analysis & Design	C
ACT211	Financial Accounting	A+
ACT211	Financial Accounting	B+
MKT311	Principles of Marketing	A
ACT212	Cost Accounting	B
ACT212	Cost Accounting	A
MIS432	Database Design	A
MGT490	Special Topics	

Listing 6.23. Query with Left Outer Join Clause

6.12. Subquery

A SELECT query can embed another SELECT query which is called **subquery**. A subquery can have its subquery, and go on. The execution sequence of the query is "from inside to outside" which means that the most interior subquery is executed first. There are two major reasons of using subquery, as explained below.

6.12.1. Subquery is alternative to join operation for special cases

A subquery can be used as an alternative to a join operation in a simple situation. Revisit the query in Listing 6.19 which is to "*list all students who receive "A" or "A+" in any course.*" One can follow the three step logic presented right before Listing 6.19, and write a subquery as shown in Listing 6.24.

```
SELECT  tblStudent.StudentName
FROM    tblStudent
WHERE   tblStudent.StudentID IN
            (SELECT tblGrading.StudentID
             FROM tblGrading
             WHERE(tblGrading.Grade='A+'
             OR tblGrading.Grade='A'));
```

StudentName
John
Robert

Listing 6.24. An Example of Subquery that Avoids Join Operation

In Listing 6.24, there are two SELECT commands. The computer performs the second SELECT command first to find student IDs who receive "A" or "A+" from tblGrading. It then finds the matched the student IDs in tblStudent (by the first WHERE clause). Finally, it performs the top SELECT command to find the corresponding student names.

The SQL query with a subquery in Listing 6.24 does the same job as the query in Listing 6.19 does, but avoids the join operation which takes significantly more computation resource than a subquery does. However, in cases where data from two or more tables are going to display concurrently, subquery becomes incapable, and a join operation must be applied.

6.12.2. Subquery is alternative to GROUP BY

A subquery can be used as an alternative to the GROUP BY clause. For example, the query in Listing 6.25(a) is to *"show each student's name along with the number of courses she/he has taken."* using a subquery.

```
SELECT tblStudent.StudentName,
    (SELECT COUNT(*)
     FROM tblGrading
     WHERE tblStudent.StudentID=tblGrading.StudentID)
     AS NumberOfCourses
FROM tblStudent;
```

StudentName	NumberOfCourses
John	3
Anne	2
Robert	3

Listing 6.25(a). Subquery for Groups

The subquery does the similar job as GROUP BY clause which is shown in Listing 6.25(b).

```
SELECT tblStudent.StudentName, COUNT(*) AS NumberOfCourses
FROM tblStudent, tblGrading
WHERE tblStudent.StudentID=tblGrading.StudentID
GROUP BY tblStudent.StudentName;
```

Listing 6.25(b). GROUP BY Clause for Groups

The use of subquery for groups could cause confusion if the design of the subquery is incorrect. For the beginner, the GROUP BY clause would be better than this type of subquery.

6.12.3. Subquery determines uncertain criteria

In many cases subquery is necessary. Suppose we want to know *"which students with ID numbers greater than '02000000' have the earliest enrollment year of such students?"* Beginners of SQL often have the following wrong answer.

```
SELECT StudentName
FROM    tblStudent
WHERE   StudentID > '02000000'
AND StudentEnrolYear = MIN(StudentEnrolYear);
```

This query does not work. The fact is that SQL does not allow an uncertain term on the right side in the WHERE clause because of its ambiguity. In the above wrong SQL, the WHERE clause is equivalent to

```
WHERE StudentEnrolYear=?
```

because MIN(StudentEnrolYear) is unknown in terms of its specific condition. To make a correct WHERE clause, you need to put either a certain value or a subquery on the right side of the WHERE clause. Thus, the correct SQL for the above query is Listing 6.26.

```
SELECT StudentName
FROM    tblStudent
WHERE   StudentID > '02000000'
AND StudentEnrolYear=
        (SELECT MIN(StudentEnrolYear)
         FROM tblStudent
         WHERE   StudentID > '02000000');
```

StudentName
Robert

Listing 6.26. An Example of Subquery for Uncertain Condition

Two points in writing subquery, which determines uncertain criteria in the WHERE clause, are worth noting.

(1) When the right side of the WHERE clause is uncertain (e.g., MIN, MAX, SUM, AVG, COUNT), you must use a subquery to replace the uncertain condition.

(2) In Listing 6.26, you can see that the condition StudentID>'02000000' in the host WHERE clause repeats in the condition in the subquery WHERE clause. If this condition is not repeated in the two WHERE clauses, then the meaning of the query is quite different. For example, if the first WEHRE clause is omitted, the query represents *"which students* (in the entire population) *have the earliest enrollment year of* those students with ID number greater than '02000000'?" On the other hand, if the second WEHRE clause is omitted, the query represents *"which students with ID numbers greater than '02000000' have the earliest enrollment year of* all *students?"*

A query can have join operations as well as subquery. Listing 6.27 is a query: *"List student names, course names, and grades of those students whose ID numbers are greater than '02000000' and have the earliest enrollment year of such students."*

```
SELECT tblStudent.StudentName,
       tblCourse.CourseName, tblGrading.Grade
FROM tblStudent, tblCourse, tblGrading
WHERE tblStudent.StudentID=tblGrading.StudentID
AND tblCourse.CourseID=tblGrading.CourseID
AND tblStudent.StudentID > '02000000'
AND tblStudent.StudentEnrolYear=
    (SELECT MIN(tblStudent.StudentEnrolYear)
     FROM tblStudent
     WHERE tblStudent.StudentID > '02000000');
```

StudentName	CourseName	Grade
Robert	Database Design	A
Robert	Cost Accounting	B
Robert	Principles of Marketing	A

Listing 6.27. An Example of Join and Subquery

Again, when you use multiple tables, qualifiers (i.e., table names) must be applied to specify the attribute names.

6.13. UNION Operator

The UNION operator connects two SELECT statements to produce all the rows that would be in query results of the first SELECT statement, the second SELECT statement, or both. The UNION operator is commonly used to create a virtual table. As an illustrative example, the query in Listing 6.28 is to *"list the course ID and course enrollment for each course that has enrollment greater than 35, or the student name and student ID for each student who enrolled after 2013."* In fact, the UNION operator is a kind of OR operator between the two SELECT statement. This example is merely to demonstrate how the UNION operator works. As shown in this example, if the attributes listed in the two SELECT statements are not comparable, the query result of the UNION operator would not be particularly meaningful.

```
SELECT CourseID AS Name, CourseEnrollment AS Data
FROM tblCourse
WHERE CourseEnrollment>35
UNION
SELECT StudentName AS Name, StudentID AS Data
FROM tblStudent
WHERE StudentEnrolYear>2013;
```

Name	Data
Anne	02345678
MIS315	40
MIS322	38

Listing 6.28. UNION Operator

6.14. Tactics for Writing Queries

The following is general tactics for writing SQL scripts in SELECT statements.

(1) Read the query carefully. Determine what data are to be retrieved and what

attributes are to be included in the SELECT command.

(2) Determine what tables are will be used in the FROM clause.

(3) If two or more tables are involved, use a join operation(s) (match the primary key in one table with the foreign key in another table) in the WHERE clause.

(4) Construct the WHERE clause by including all conditions that are linked by AND or OR. Never use any aggregate function in the WHERE clause directly.

(5) If a condition has an uncertain criterion (MAX, MIN, AVG, SUM, COUNT) on the right side of the condition, use subquery.

(6) Consider GROUP BY (for each group) with HAVING condition, ORDER BY clauses, and other operators (e.g., DISTINCT) if needed.

(7) For hands-on practices, you may construct test tables with a limited number of test samples to test the SQL script to see if it generates the expected result.

6.15. SQL Embedded in Host Computer Programming Languages

Computer application programs in large languages (e.g., COBOL, C++, Java, and .NET) often host SQL scripts to deal with relational databases directly. These programs, typically called middleware, retrieve the needed data through the SQL scripts, and then perform complicated manipulations on the retrieved data for the business applications.

To make a connection to the databases and process the embedded SQL, specific database connection software must be integrated into the system, as further discussed in Chapter 9. Listing 6.29 is an example of Web application that uses SQL to access Microsoft Access database in the ADO.NET environment. In this example, the Access database is named TestDB.accdb that is stored in the same folder with the ASP.NET program on the server. The code in bold is relevant to the use of SQL to search data from tblStudent by the user on the client side on the Internet. Figure 6.3 shows the execution result in the Microsoft Visual Studio environment.

```
<%@ Page Language="VB" %>
<%@ import Namespace="System.Data.OleDb" %>
<script runat="server">
    Public Sub Page_Load()
```

```
    End Sub
    Public Sub abc(sender As Object, e As EventArgs)
    label1.text="The inquired record for " + textbox1.value + " is:"
    dim dbconn,sql,dbcomm,dbread
    dim var1 as String
    var1=textbox1.value
    dbconn=New OleDbConnection("Provider=Microsoft.ACE.OLEDB.12.0; _
            data source=" & server.mappath("TestDB.accdb"))
    dbconn.Open()
    sql="SELECT * FROM tblStudent WHERE StudentID=" & "'" & var1 & "'"
    dbcomm=New OleDbCommand(sql,dbconn)
    dbread=dbcomm.ExecuteReader()
    tblStudent.DataSource=dbread
    tblStudent.DataBind()
    dbread.Close()
    dbconn.Close()
    End Sub
</script>
<html><body><form runat="server">
        Type the student number for inquiry:
        <input id="textbox1" type="text" runat="server" /><br />
        <input id="submit1" type="submit" value="Search"
            runat="server" onserverclick="abc" /><br /><br />
        <asp:Label id="label1" runat="server"></asp:Label>
        <asp:Repeater id="tblStudent" runat="server">
            <HeaderTemplate><table border="1" width="100%">
                <tr><th>Student ID</th>
                    <th>Student Name</th>
                    <th>Student Address</th>
                    <th>Student Enrollment Year</th></tr>
            </HeaderTemplate>
            <ItemTemplate>
             <tr><td><%#Container.DataItem("StudentID")%></td>
                <td><%#Container.DataItem("StudentName")%></td>
                <td><%#Container.DataItem("StudentAddress")%></td>
                <td><%#Container.DataItem("StudentEnrolYear")%></td></tr>
            </ItemTemplate>
            <FooterTemplate></table></FooterTemplate>
        </asp:Repeater>
    </form>
</body></html>
```

Listing 6.29. SQL Is Used in ADO.NET

Figure 6.3. Search Access Database in the Internet Environment

The format of SQL scripts in a host computer programming language depends on the syntax of the host language. As you can see in Listing 6.29, in the .NET environment, a SQL script is a text string, and is placed between the double quotation mark pairs which are linked by "&" signs. Note that an unnecessary space sign in the SQL script could cause problems in compiling the program. Also, each database connection open and close cycle can execute only one SQL script. In other words, if there are multiple SQL scripts in a program, the server must open and close the database connection multiple times.

Chapter 6 Exercises

1.* Consider the following tables in the GreenHeating database in exercise question 2 of chapter 3.

HOUSE

*HouseAddress	HouseOwner	Insurance

HEATINGUNIT

*HeathingUnitID	UnitName	UnitType	Manufactory
	DateOfBuilt	Capacity	HouseAddress

TECHNICIAN

*EmployeeNumber	EmployeeName	Title	YearHired

SERVICE

*HeatingUnitID	*EmployeeNumber	ServiceType	*Date	*Time

a) Find the owner of the house "285 Westport Rd".

b) List the heating unit names and numbers of the gas heating units which was built in house "285 Westport Rd".

c) List the heating unit number, date of built, manufactory, and all types of gas, electric, and solar with capacity between 3000 and 4000 cub-feet from largest to smallest.

d) List the names of technicians who maintained a heating unit in "285 Westport Rd" along with the service type performed.

e) Find the name and number of the largest Gas heating unit.

Minicase: *GreenJetNB (Chapter 6)*

Follow the GreenJetNB minicase in Chapter 3. Suppose the GreenJetNB database has the following tables.

AIRCRAFT

*AircraftID	AircraftModel	Capacity	DateOfBuilt	MaxFlyDistance

PILOT

*PilotID	PilotName	Gender	DateOfBirth			
			DateOfHire	CellPhone	Salary	

PASSENGER

*PassengerID	PassengerName	PassengerAddress	PassengerPhone

FLIGHT

*FlightID	*FlightDate	DepartureAirport	DepartureTime		
	ArrivalAirport	ArrivalTime	*AircraftID*	*PilotID*	

TRIP

PassengerID	*FlightID*	*FlightDate*	Airfare	
	ReservationDate	SatisfactionRating		

Write SQL for the following queries.

a) Create the PASSENGER table using the assumed data types for the attributes.
b) Follow Question a. Insert a record into the PASSENGER table using assumed values of these attributes.
c) Follow Question b. Change the passenger name of the record you have inserted to the table.
d) Follow Question b. Delete the record you have inserted to the table.
e) Delete the PASSENGER table.

f) List the names and telephone numbers of all of the pilots.

g) List the aircrafts that have at least 30 passenger seats and were built after 2005. Order the results from smallest to largest.

h) Find the aircraft records (including all available data) for those aircrafts in which the model names begin with 'Wind'.

i) List the names of the female pilots who were hired after 2005 and whose salaries are greater than 100000.

j) How many pilots are working for the company?

k) Find the total number of trips for each passenger, and only list passengers (PassengerID) who have had at least 3 trips.

l) Find the total number of trips for each passenger, and only list passengers (PassengerID) who have a satisfaction rating of 3 or lower.

m) List the names of the pilots who have taken to the air between New Bedford and Providence.

n) List the names of the passengers who have commuted between New Bedford and Providence.

o) List the names of the pilots who were hired after 2005 and have the highest salary in such a group of pilots.

p) List the names of the pilots who were hired after 2005 and have the highest salary of all pilots.

CHAPTER 7. PHYSICAL DATABASE DESIGN

7.1. Physical Design

The normalization process and the database logical design ensure that the database contains no redundant data, and maintain data consistency and integrity. However, a database with a logical design only can have disadvantages of poor performance. For instance, in the database represented by Figure 3.13, suppose students access the STUDENT table and the TEACH table together frequently during the course registration period, the join operations might take place frequently. As a result, the database would have slow response to the concurrent accesses of hundreds or even thousands users. To improve the performance of the database, one might design the database to perform the following operations so that the database would have quick response to the users' requests without scarifying data accuracy to a certain degree.

(1) Select currently registered students' records from the huge STUDENT table, and temporarily store them as a separate table, say, STUDENT-CURRENT.

(2) Join the STUDENT-CURRENT table and the TEACH table, and temporarily store the joined table on the disk as a separate table, say STUDENT-CURRENT-TEACH.

(3) Use the STUDENT-CURRENT-TEACH table for the registration period, so that repeating join operations can be eliminated. After the period, discharge these two temporary tables.

Physical database design is to supplement the logical database design and to improve the database performance in the following aspects.

- **Response time** – the time delay from the database access request to the result appears;
- **Throughput volume** – the volume of data access output in a given time period;
- **Security** – the data protection.

In the early years of database (1970s and 1980s), physical database design mainly deals with the data structure of the database at the physical storage level. In the context of contemporary databases, physical database design has a broad range of techniques. In many cases, a physical database design alters the logical database design. Note that those modifications to the logical database design should be well controlled by the DBMS. The data integrity, accuracy, and timeliness might be compromised due to the physical design (e.g., temporary data redundancy), but such drawbacks should not have any serious consequence in the specific business environment.

Unlike logical database design, physical database design is more or less artistic and depends upon the specific situations of applications of the database. The support functions for physical database design vary depending on the DBMS. Large DBMS such as Oracle and DB2 have rich functionalities for physical database design, but end user oriented DBMS for tiny databases, such as Microsoft Access, have few physical design features. In this chapter, ten important physical database design techniques are discussed.

7.2. Adding Index

As explained in Chapter 2, a large database has massive B-trees so that random searches would be fast. All primary keys are automatically indexed by B-trees by the DBMS. However, if the values of a non-key attribute (or a combination of attributes) are often used for random search, then this attribute should be also indexed. For example, if the user searches students from the STUDENT table often by StudentName as well, then StudentName should have an index although it is not the primary key. The downside of adding indexes is the increase of computation overhead for the maintenance of B-trees.

7.3. Adding Subschema

An ER diagram represents the database's **schema** which is the conceptual semantic structure of the entire database. A **subschema** is a virtual part of the database which is created for a particular purpose (e.g., for a user or a group of users). Using a subschema, the user is only allowed to use the part of the database within her/his subschema, and is not even aware of the existence of the other part of the database. A subschema is an important device in protecting the security and privacy of data. It can also improve the performance of query processing. A **view** is a special case of subschema with one virtual table which is a saved query result. The virtual table assembles parts from the database tables in response to the frequent query. Figure 7.1 illustrates subschema. The downside of adding subschemata is the increase of computation resources consumption.

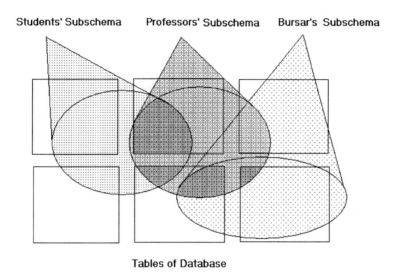

Students' Subschema   Professors' Subschema   Bursar's Subschema

Tables of Database

Figure 7.1. Subschemata

7.4. Clustering Tables

If two or more tables are used together so often, these tables should be clustered; that is, are placed close each to other (e.g., on the same disk cylinder) so that the computer access device can retrieve the data from these tables together quickly. For instance, if the STUDENT table is often accessed together with the COURSE table, then the two tables should be physically placed closely (e.g., on the adjacent cylinders). The downside of clustering is that it might increase the "distances" between one of the clustered tables and other tables which are not in the cluster because it is impossible to cluster all tables together.

7.5. Merging Tables

If two or more tables are repeatedly joined through the join operations, then **merging** these tables into a large table might be necessary to reduce the valuable computing time spent on the repeating join operations. The example in the first section of this chapter explains this technique. The **combined table** becomes a **denormalized** table and usually contains data redundancy. In principle, the DBMS should keep the original copies of the normalized tables, and use the combined table for only a period. To keep the data sufficiently accurate, re-merging could take place from time to time. In comparison with clustering tables, merging tables is short-lived measures for easing repeating join operations.

7.6. Horizontal Partitioning Table

In **horizontal partitioning**, the rows of a table are divided into parts, and the parts are stored separately for many reasons, such as the different access frequencies of the parts and the different security requirements of the parts. For instance, if the STUDENT table is huge, it can be divided into two parts based on the values of StudentYear: one sub-table contains records of active students and the other sub-table contains records of inactive students (e.g., alumni) (see Figure 7.2). The sub-table of active students is used more often. Because of the smaller size, the join operations are less time consuming. The downside of partitioning is that the computation overhead would be increase when the entire table is used.

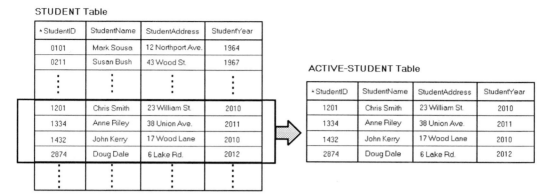

Figure 7.2. Horizontal Partitioning Table

7.7. Vertical Partitioning Table

In **vertical partitioning**, the columns of a table are divided into parts, and the parts are stored separately because the different applications frequently require different attributes. For example, suppose the STUDENT table is often used by academic advisors as well as the Residence Office. Advisors access StudentID, StudentName, and StudentYear frequently, but do not access StudentAddress often. On the other hand, the Residence Office accesses StudentName and StudentAddress frequently, but do not really use other data. In the new academic seasons, the database might divide the huge STUDENT table into two sub-tables, and each sub-table has its own attributes in response to the high usage of the STUDENT data. Note that, when creating vertical partitioning, each part must have a copy of the primary key. In this example, one sub-table contains StudentID, StudentName, and StudentYear; and the other sub-table contains StudentID, StudentName, and StudentAddress (see Figure 7.3).

The concepts of vertical partitioning and adding indexes are different, although both involve attributes. The adding index technique is applied to situations of quick search by a specific attribute, while the vertical partitioning technique is applied to situations of retrieving all values of specific attributes together.

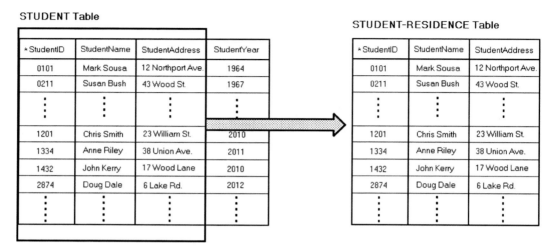

Figure 7.3. Vertical Partitioning Table

7.8. Creating New Primary Key

Combination primary keys make data retrieval process slower, especially when the combination key involves too many attributes, such as the example in Figure 3.13 [StudentID+CourseID+ProfessorID]. Such a combination key makes indexing in the B-trees tedious. It is preferred to create a new single attribute as the primary key for the table to replace the combination primary key, but the table still keeps the attributes of the original combination key because they are either foreign keys or intersection data. For instance, one may create a new primary key, say OccurrenceID, to replace [StudentID+CourseID+ProfessorID]. However, StudentID, CourseID, and ProfessorID will stay in the associative entity as the foreign keys from other tables.

7.9. Substituting Foreign Key

A foreign key of the table on the M-side is usually the primary key of the table on the 1-side. However, if an alternative key of the table on the 1-side is more often used for data retrieval than the primary key, this alternative key could be used as the foreign key of the table on the M-side. For instance, in the database represented by Figure 3.13, ProfessorID is the foreign key in the TEACH relation. Considering ProfessorName is an alternative key of the PROFESSOR relation, and is used more frequently than ProfessorID, ProfessorName can substitute ProfessorID as the foreign key in the TEACH relation. In such a way, the preferred combination data of ProfessorName, CourseID, and Responsibility can be retrieved quickly from the single TEACH table without involving the PROFESSOR table.

7.10. Duplicating Table or Parts of Partitioned Table

When multiple users try to access the same table, the response time of the database will be slow. To reduce the bottleneck effect (traffic jam), the technique of **duplicating tables** (or duplicating parts of partitioned tables) is used to route different queries to the different copies. For instance, if the STUDENT table is accessed intensively during a certain period, it can have duplicated copies to response numerous queries at the same time. Apparently, duplication creates the risk of overt data redundancy. The duplication should be temporary for the access peak hours, and should be fully managed by the DBMS.

7.11. Storing Information (Processed Data)

As discussed earlier in this book, a database is not an information base and it stores raw data only. In principle, the computer processes the raw data to provide the needed information (or processed data, or derived data), such as summation, average, and trend, upon the user's request. However, if a piece of information is requested frequently and/or by many users in a short period, the system would waste much computation resource to reproduce needed information. **Storing information** (or **processed data**) is to reduce the unnecessarily repeating computation. Apparently, the stored piece of information should be of short life to keep the information updated. For example, the GPA is not supposed to be stored in the STUDENT table, because the GPA is redundant if all grades for a student are already recorded in the database. However, during the advising period, the GPA of a student is frequently needed. To avoid the repeating calculation of GPA, the STUDENT table might store the GPA. Clearly, the GPA is redundant, and must be re-calculated or be inaccurate once a new grade is recorded.

7.12. Implementation of Physical Database Design

The implementation of physical database design highly depends on the DBMS. A sophisticated DBMS has **DBMS performance tuning**, a set of algorithms and procedures designed to improve the database performance. Generally, several methods available in many DBMSs can be used for the implementation of physical database design.

(1) **Storage-related construction**. Many large DBMSs allow the DBA to define storage groups for tables when constructing the database. This makes it possible to cluster tables.

(2) **SQL-related construction**. Many large DBMSs support advanced SQL for physical database design. These DBMSs allows the DBA or users of the database to implement the physical database design through commands such as CREATE INDEX, CREATE TABLE, ALTER TABLE, CREATE VIEW, and CREATE SCHEMA. These SQL-related constructions make a physical design possible to add indexes, to change the structure of tables, to make duplications or partitions, and to create views or subschemata.

(3) **Query optimizer**. Many DBMSs support the SQL ANALYZE command to analyze database performance statistics. Also, a sophisticated DBMS has its own algorithms for determine the most efficient way to execute SQL. The DBA can define the mode of the query optimization: either rule-based or cost-based.

Chapter 7 Exercises

1.* Consider the following tables in the GreenHeating database in exercise question 2 of chapter 3.

HOUSE

*HouseAddress	HouseOwner	Insurance

HEATINGUNIT

*HeathingUnitID	UnitName	UnitType	Manufactory
	DateOfBuilt	Capacity	*HouseAddress*

TECHNICIAN

*EmployeeNumber	EmployeeName	Title	YearHired

SERVICE

HeatingUnitID	*EmployeeNumber*	ServiceType	*Date	*Time

Analyze each of the following situations, and state what physical database design technique you would like to apply to improve the data processing performance.

a) There is a critical need to quickly list the heating units with a particular type.

b) There is a frequent need to list all heating unit numbers along with their unit types and houses.

c) There is a frequent need to retrieve detailed data about a heating unit together with detailed data about the house in which it locates.

d) There is a much more frequent and high priority need to access the records for Gas heating units than for the other types.

e) Due to large numbers of access activity, the HEATINGUNIT relation has become a bottleneck.

Minicase: *GreenJetNB (Chapter 7)*

Follow the GreenJetNB minicase in Chapter 3. Suppose the GreenJetNB database has the following tables.

AIRCRAFT

*AircraftID	AircraftModel	Capacity	DateOfBuilt	MaxFlyDistance

PILOT

*PilotID	PilotName	Gender	DateOfBirth			
			DateOfHire	CellPhone	Salary	

PASSENGER

*PassengerID	PassengerName	PassengerAddress	PassengerPhone

FLIGHT

*FlightID	*FlightDate	DepartureAirport	DepartureTime		
	ArrivalAirport	ArrivalTime	*AircraftID*	*PilotID*	

TRIP

PassengerID	*FlightID*	*FlightDate*	Airfare	
	ReservationDate	SatisfactionRating		

Analyze each of the following independent situations, and apply physical database design techniques to improve performance.

a) There is a critical need to quickly list the flights that uses a particular airport.

b) Users of operation are not allowed to access pilots' private data which are used by the human resource department only.

c) There is a frequent need to be able to retrieve detailed data about a flight together with detailed data about its passengers.

d) There is a frequent need to get a list of the names and phone numbers of the passengers together with the data of their trips including flight number, flight date, and satisfaction ratings.

e) There is a much more frequent and high priority need to access the records of the flights on holidays than other flight records.

f) In the TRIP table, there is a frequent need with strict response time requirements for accessing the flight number together with the passenger number and satisfaction rating than for accessing the rest of the data in the table.

g) In the TRIP table, there is a frequent need with strict response time requirements for accessing the record(s) of a particular combination of flight number, passenger number, and satisfaction rating.

h) Consider the TRIP table. The database designer wants to create a table called SATISFACTION that records more passengers' satisfaction data beyond just SatisfactionRating.

i) Assume that the PassengerName attribute in the PASSENGER table is unique. There is a frequent need to quickly retrieve the following data about trips: passenger name, flight number, flight date, airfare, and reservation date.

j) Due to a large number of users, the FLIGHT relation has become a bottleneck of the database access traffic.

k) Due to a large number of users, the records of the flights on holidays have become a bottleneck of the database access traffic.

l) There is a frequent need to quickly find the total number of trips that any particular passenger has traveled with GreenJetNB.

CHAPTER 8. DATABASE ADMINISTRATION

This chapter describes the major functions of database administration, and the major responsibilities and tasks of the DBA.

8.1. Data Planning and Database Design

Data are valuable assets for the organization. It is crucial for the organization to plan what data are needed for the time being, as well as in the future. The DBA should play a leading role in data planning, database design, as well as choosing the DBMS.

8.2. Data Coordination

Data are the shared corporate resource. Whether and how **centralize** or **decentralize** the data in the organization are always questions without clear-cut answers. The DBA should coordinate the use of data as well as the distribution of the computational costs for the organization.

8.3. Data Security, Access Policies, and Data Ownership

Data security, data privacy, and data ethics become more and more important for the organization. The DBA plays key role in designing the **access policies** for the organization, and monitors the execution of these policies to maintain the standards in data security, data privacy, and data ethics. The database administration acts as the custodian of the data of the organization, and should clarify the **ownerships** of the data.

8.4. Data Quality

Data quality is evaluated by accuracy, objectivity, believability, reputation, access, security, relevancy, value-added, timeliness, completeness, amount of data, interpretability, ease of understanding, concise representation, and consistent representation. The DBA should apply the concepts and tools of **total data quality control** in managing the data resource.

8.5. Database Performance

The DBA should monitor the performance of the database and should lead the specialist team of the organization to improve the database performance.

8.6. User Training

User training is another important task for the DBA in many organizations. All users of the database, including programmers and end users, need to know the policies, procedures, design, standards, and utilities of the database.

8.7. Data Standards, Data Dictionary, and Documentation

A database has its **standards** to regulate the names of tables and attributes, data types of attributes, and procedures/methods of the use of the database. If the company becomes a member of an EDI group or an association, the database might have to adopt new data standards.

A tool for enforcing data standards for databases is **data dictionary**. A data dictionary stores **metadata**, namely data about the data in the database. For instance, suppose a database has two tables as shown in the upper part of Figure 8.1. A simple data dictionary of this database looks like the table in the lower part of Figure 8.1.

There is no universal standard for data dictionary. Individual DBMS has the data dictionary in its own way. A **passive data dictionary** is used for **documentation** purposes. The passive data dictionary is simply a small-scale database for the administration of the "mother database". An **active data dictionary** is a sophisticated one that interacts with the "mother database" in a real-time fashion. If the "mother database" has a change, the data dictionary is automatically changed correspondingly, and also might provide consulting information to the administration regarding the change. On the other hand, if the data dictionary has a change, the change will trigger changes to the "mother database".

In Technical Guide II of this textbook for using Microsoft Access, you can find a way to retrieve the Access DMBS generated data dictionary for the database in Microsoft Access. If you build a database for your course project, you can learn a variety of metadata that are useful for the database management.

"Mother Database"

CLASSROOM Relation			
* ClassroomID	ClassroomLocation	ClassroomType	ClassroomSize

COURSE Relation			
* CourseID	CourseName	CourseEnrollment	CourseTime	*ClassroomID*

Data Dictionary

Relations Metadata

Table Name	Number of Records	Disk Cylinder	Access Permission code
CLASSROOM	232	A234	103
COURSE	568	M467	347

Attributes Metadata

Attribute Name	Data Type	Attribute Length	Indexed	Validation Rule Code
ClassroomID	Text	6	Key / FK	12
ClassroomLocation	Text	10	No	23
ClassroomType	Text	10	No	23
ClassroomSize	Number	3	No	35
CourseID	Text	6	Key	12
CourseName	Text	30	Yes	23
CourseEnrollment	Number	3	No	35
CourseTime	Date/Time	16	No	11

Figure 8.1. Example of Data Dictionary

8.8. Database Backup and Recovery

A database can be destroyed by a disaster, or can be corrupted after a failure of hardware or software, or can have errors caused by human mistakes. The DBA should have a database **backup and recovery** strategy and disaster planning for the database. There have been many backup and recovery techniques that are commonly supported by DBMS. Three major backup and recovery methods are described below.

8.8.1. Mirrored databases

The easiest backup and recovery strategy is to use of **mirrored** (or **duplicated**) databases for the database system. Two or even three copies of the entire database are maintained concurrently. Physically, the duplicated copies of database should be placed in different places. If any of the duplicated databases goes wrong, simply use other one as the backup copy to recover the damaged one. Apparently, this backup and recovery method is prohibitively expensive if the database is huge. It might be useful in military or space projects, but is rarely used in business.

8.8.2. Re-do transactions

In the **re-do transactions** approach, the database is taken a "snapshot" periodically to have a backup copy. After the backup, the database system keeps all **logs** (or **journals**) that record every transaction occurred after the backup. Once the database is damaged, the last database backup copy and the logs after the last backup are used to re-produce a new database. This process is illustrated in Figure 8.2. The backup and recovery processes can be done automatically by the DBMS. Usually, at least three generations of backup copies along with the logs are reserved for the database system.

8.8.3. Un-do transactions

A damage in the database can be caused by erroneous operations (e.g., human mistakes), or by incompletely processed transactions. In such cases, the scope of the damage is small, and the re-do transactions method is still too expensive. The **un-do transactions** method is designed to solve those situations. In the un-do transactions method, the system keeps logs as backup. Once error occurs, the logs and the erroneous database are used by the DBMS to un-do the incomplete/flawed transactions to correct the database. The invalid erroneous or incomplete transactions are then reviewed with human intervene. The un-do transactions method is illustrated in Figure 8.3.

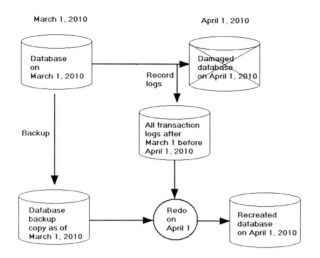

Figure 8.2. Re-Do Transactions for Recovery

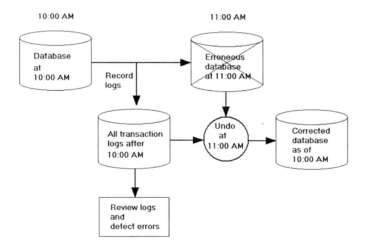

Figure 8.3. Un-Do Transactions for Recovery

8.9. Data Archiving

The organization needs data retention for particular needs and/or legal reasons. There have been many business laws or government laws that specify the data retention requirements. One solution to data retention is **data archiving**. A data archive is a place where a set of certain data is kept. Typically, the archive does not belong to the database itself, but should be traceable from the database.

8.10. Database Maintenance

The database of the organization needs maintenance due to hardware and software upgrading and/or other changes in the environment. The DBA should have long-term maintenance policies as well as short-term maintenance plans, and have the responsibility of dealing with cost issues and the relationships with vendors for database maintenance.

8.11. Managing Business Rules Related to the Database Design

A **business rule** is a statement that aims to influence or guide business in the organization. Business rule management is critical for business success, but is under-researched in the IT field because it involves so many areas including business regulation, organization structure, job responsibility, business procedure, security, database, and others. One of the DBA roles is to manage the business rules related to the database design. We have learned three major types of business rules for database design.

(1) Functional dependencies between the attributes of entities.

(2) Cardinalities and modalities attached to the relationships between the entities.

(3) Referential integrity rules for record insertion and deletion.

Chapter 8 Exercises

Minicase: *GreenJetNB (Chapter 8)*

Follow the GreenJetNB minicase described in Chapter 3.

1. Write a simple data dictionary (similar to Figure 8.1) for the following three tables of the GreenJetNB database.

AIRCRAFT

*AircraftID	AircraftModel	Capacity	DateOfBuilt	MaxFlyDistance

PILOT

*PilotID	PilotName	Gender	DateOfBirth			
			DateOfHire	CellPhone	Salary	

FLIGHT

*FlightID	*FlightDate	DepartureAirport	DepartureTime		
	ArrivalAirport	ArrivalTime	*AircraftID*	*PilotID*	

2. Describe a scenario that the re-do transactions method is applicable for backup and recovery of the GreenJetNB database.

3. Describe a scenario that the un-do transactions method is applicable for backup and recovery of the GreenJetNB database.

CHAPTER 9. DATABASE IN COMPUTER NETWORKS

9.1. Centralized Database in the Local Area Network Environment

A **local area network** (**LAN**) is a network that links computers and printers together. Typically, a computer with a larger computational capacity, called **server**, holds a **centralized database**, and other smaller PCs, called **clients**, use the centralized database, as illustrated in Figure 9.1. A centralized database is easy to manage, but causes data access traffic on the network if many clients use the centralized database. The DBMS of the centralized database on LAN has interface with the LAN operating system.

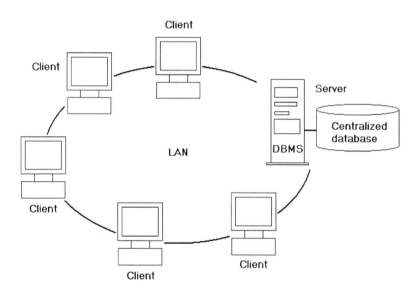

Figure 9.1. Centralized Database on LAN

9.2. Centralized Database in the Internet Environment

Massive client-server networks are connected and build the **Internet** (or **World Wide Web**). The access to a database on the Internet becomes complicated because of so many different computer hardware/software platforms and so many types of DBMS.

Also, the data security issues become more important. A general architecture of the entire system for accessing centralized database on the Internet is illustrated in Figure 9.2. The major components that are relevant to database are described below.

- **Firewall** is a computer with special software to protect the Web server, database server, and the database from unauthorized access, viruses, and other suspicious incoming code.

- **Web server** stores the Web portal, processes all applications such as order process and payment, and makes all responses to the Internet users' requests. To support applications, a Web server has three important software components: API, middleware, and ODBC.

- **API** (**Application Program Interface**) is a set of functions that allow data exchange between the application software and the database.

- **Middleware** is specialized software to access the database. The application program in Listing 6.29 is an example of middleware ADO.NET.

- **ODBC** (**Open Database Connectivity**) is software interface to relational databases. On a computer of the Windows platform, you can set ODBC for a particular relational database (e.g., SQL Server) or tabular data (e.g., Excel) through [**Administrative Tools**] in the [**Control Panel**] of [**Settings**] (see Figure 9.3). In the Java platform, **JDBC** (**Java Database Connectivity**) plays the similar role.

- **Database server** is the dedicated server for data retrieval and maintenance of the database.

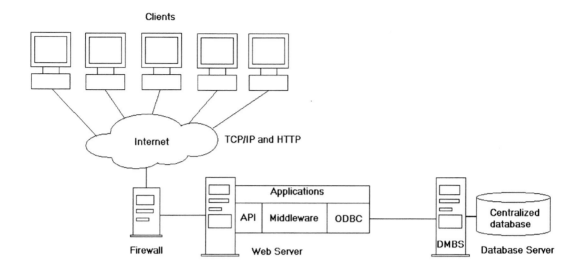

Figure 9.2. System Architecture for Accessing Database on the Internet

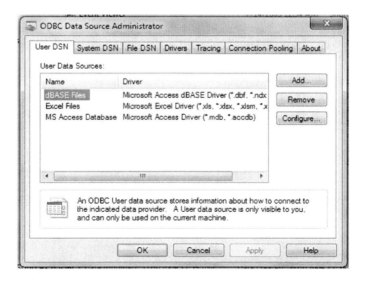

Figure 9.3. Set ODBC in Windows

9.3. Distributed Databases

A centralized database has disadvantages. First, it leads to busy network traffic. Second, the database server can never be fast enough if many users access it, and can become a bottleneck site. Third, if the centralized database goes down, all users have to wait. **Distributed databases** (see Figure 9.4) overcome these problems, and have many advantages including local autonomy, communication cost saving, and 24/7 service. However, a distributed database needs a sophisticated **distributed DBMS** (**DDBMS**) to support the complex functions.

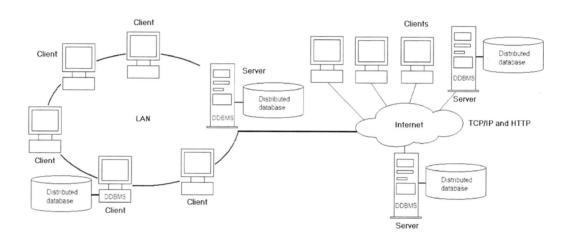

Figure 9.4. Distributed Database

9.3.1. Location transparency

The users of the distributed database just want to obtain needed data from the database, but are not interested in where the data are stored. The DDBMS takes care of data physical locations and data migration, and makes the users feel the database is centralized in somewhere. This property of distributed databases is called **location transparency**.

9.3.2. Data deployment

In the distributed database environment, physical database design becomes more important and, at the same time, more artistic. Partitioning and duplication in addition to placement are the major techniques used in **data deployment** on the network.

(1) **Partitioning** – A table may be split up into **fragments** through **horizontal partitioning**, **vertical partitioning**, or the combination of horizontal and vertical partitioning. Each **fragment** is subject to placement, as explained next.

(2) **Placement** – A table or a fragment of table should be placed at the site where the table or the fragment is used most frequently, and the site takes the major responsibility for its data integrity control as well as backup and recovery, which is called local autonomy.

(3) **Duplication** – A table or a fragment of table may have a replicated copy at the site where the table is used frequently.

The following example illustrates the concept of data deployment.

> *GreenAppliance Retail Company has the database as described in Figure 9.5(a). Its headquarters is set in Boston. There are four region offices: Providence, Toronto, New York, and Seattle. Each region office manages dozens branches in the region. Each region sells unique products. The CEOs of the company monitor the sales across the company on the daily basis, and also make decisions on the selection of suppliers regularly. The senior managers of each region office take the responsibility of sales and the performance of its branches, but do not deal with the suppliers directly. What is your strategy of deployment of the tables for the distributed database?*

The database design is shown in Figure 9.5. First of all, you must make assumptions because the provided information of the situation may be incomplete.

Then, you need to apply the physical design techniques to each table for each site of the network to address the situations of the distributed database. Two tools can be useful for articulating data deployment strategies: data deployment matrix and data deployment graph. Table 9.1 shows a data deployment matrix for the above example, and Figure 9.6 shows a data deployment graph for this distributed database.

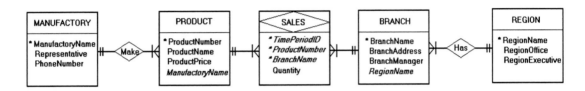

Figure 9.5. The Database of the Example

Locations Tables	Headquarters Boston	Region Offices Toronto, Miami, Seattle, Providence
MANUFACTORY	The table is placed in Boston.	
BRANCH	The table is placed in Boston.	
REGION	The table is placed in Boston.	
PRODUCT	The table is placed in Boston.	A duplicated horizontally partitioned part is placed in each region. The H.P. is based on the values of ProductNumber that are related to the region through SALES and BRANCH.
SALES	A duplicated table is placed in Boston which merges the four segments of the horizontally partitioned parts of the four regions.	A horizontally partitioned part is placed in each region. The H.P. is based on the values of BranchName that are related to the region through BRANCH.

Table 9.1. Data Deployment Matrix for Distributed Database

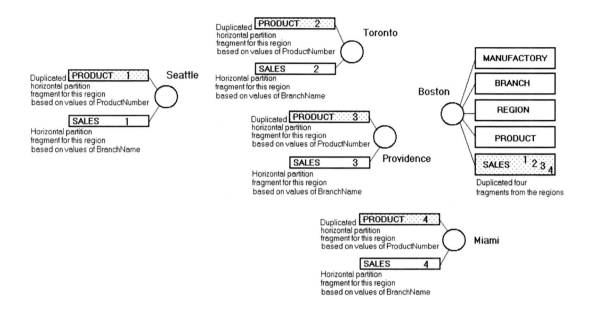

Figure 9.6. Data Deployment Graph for Distributed Database

The following is the justification of the data deployment in the above example.
(1) The REGION and BRANCH tables are mainly used by the headquarters and are rarely used by any region office. Thus, these two tables are placed in Boston.

(2) As the headquarters makes decisions on suppliers, the MANUFACTORY table is placed in Boston. Region offices might access the MANUFACTORY table occasionally, but the usage is low since they do not assume the responsibility of selection of suppliers.

(3) As each region office takes the responsibility of sales and its performance, the SALES table should be horizontally partitioned for each region office based on the values of BranchName that are related to the values of RegionName through the BRANCH table. The individual sub-table is placed to the corresponding region office.

The headquarters also needs to access the SALES table on the daily basis but not in the real-time mode. Thus, a duplication SALES table, which merges the four sub-tables for the four region offices, is placed in Boston.

(4) As the headquarters takes the responsibility of selection of suppliers, the PRODUCT table is placed in Boston. However, each region office must access the PRODUCT table as well for monitoring sales activities. As each region sells unique products, the PRODUCT table is duplicated for each region office for only a horizontally partitioned part which is relevant to the products for that region. Note that the horizontal partition of the PRODUCT table for each region office is based on the values of ProductNumber that are related to the values of RegionName though the SALES table and the BRANCH table.

9.3.3. Data integrity control

As duplicated data spread in many places, data integrity control becomes complicated. Also, **concurrency control** in distributed databases becomes especially important and difficult. Additional layer of concurrency control procedures are implemented in DDMBS.

9.3.4. Distributed join operations

Join operations in distributed databases would become more time consuming because the joined tables may not be located in the same place. Many heuristic algorithms are employed to "optimize" **distributed join operations**.

9.4. XML for Databases

XML (Extensible Markup Language) is a computer language designed to provide a standard information description framework used for data exchanges on the Internet. XML and HTML both are derived from the **Standard Generalized Markup language (SGML)** which was defined in 1986 as an international standard for document markup. XML was completed in early 1998 by **Word Wide Web Consortium** (W3C). However, the implementation of the XML standard is far from over and depends upon the progress of the entire information technology industry.

Also, the XML technology is somehow more complicated than any other computer language.

The major motivation of the use of XML is the need for uniform data format for data exchanges among different databases on the Internet. There have been many database systems commonly used in the information industry. Although SQL is a standard language for databases, the data formats are all platform-dependent. To transfer data from one database to another, usually one needs an interface implemented by computer programs to describe the specific data formats (see Figure 9.7).

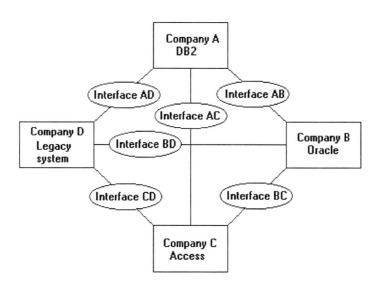

Figure 9.7. Data Exchanges between Databases Could Be Complicated

To make data transfers on the Internet efficient, we need a common data format description framework so that each database can understand exactly what is requested or what is received. The price for this is that each database must support the XML standard (so called XML-enabled database) in order to exchange data in the common

XML format (see Figure 9.8).

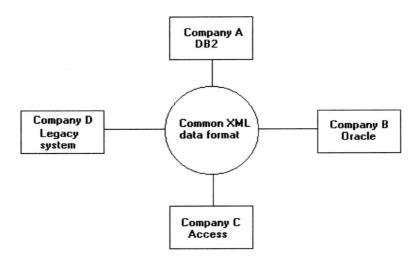

Figure 9.8. The Common XML Data Format Makes Data Exchanges Efficient

Furthermore, the traditional relational databases are typically used for processing numerical data and character data. However, the data types available on the Internet are rich, including image, audio, video, complex documents, and international characters. Using XML, these rich data formats can be easily handled.

Listing 9.1 shows an example of an XML document for the STUDENT table in Figure 6.2. As you can see from this example, the user can search the data in the XML document by using the names of tables and attributes which are specified in the XML tags.

It is worth noting several important points about XML and its companion tools.

(1) The XML data model is hierarchical, not relational. The conversion of data from a relational database into the XML format might not be as straightforward as people thought.

(2) An XML document is actually a datasheet that can be used for data search because each piece of data is described by tags. However, an XML document cannot be used

for data presentation directly. To present data in an XML document, one must use another computer language, such as XSLT or CSS, for data retrieval and presentation. (3) An XML document contains the data that can be shared by a group of users on the Internet. Thus, the structure of the XML document must be well-formatted, otherwise no one can really understand. Thus, one must use another computer language, such as XML Schema or DTD, to validate the structure of the XML document.

In summary, to fully use XML, one must apply at least two XML companion computer languages: one for data retrieval and presentation, and the other for validation.

```
<?xml version="1.0" standalone="yes"?>
<StudentTable>
 <Student
      StudentID="01234567"
      StudentName="John"
      StudentAddress="285 Westport"
      StudentEnrolYear="2012" >
 </Student>
 <Student
      StudentID="02345678"
      StudentName="Anne"
      StudentAddress="287 Eastport"
      StudentEnrolYear="2014" >
 </Student>
 <Student
      StudentID="03456789"
      StudentName="Robert"
      StudentAddress="324 Northport"
      StudentEnrolYear="2013" >
 </Student>
</StudentTable>
```

Listing 9.1. XML Document for the STUDENT Table in Figure 6.2

Chapter 9 Exercises

Minicase: *GreenJetNB (Chapter 9)*

Recall the GreenJetNB minicase in Chapter 3, and the tables you developed for the GreenJetNB database for Chapter 4 and Chapter 5.

GreenJetNB is a regional airline. It has several aircrafts and various commute itineraries between hubs and small cities. The GreenJetNB's database keeps data of aircraft, pilots, past and future flights, passengers who traveled with GreenJetNB, aircraft maintenance work, and sales of airtickets.

1. GreenJetNB has decided to reconFigure T2-he database as a distributed database, and to deploy the data in four major airports: New Bedford (MA) (also GreenJetNB's headquarters), New Haven (CT), Burlington (VT), and Bangor (ME). Data are supposed to be distributed and replicated among these four locations. The data have the following main characteristics:

(1) The data of aircrafts, pilots, schedules, and airticket sales are processed in the headquarters.

(2) The regular maintenance jobs for each aircraft are performed at a major airport except for emergency situations.

(3) The passenger data are available at the four major airports so that the adjacent small airports access the data for passenger check-in and check-out.

Design a distributed relational database for GreenJetNB by showing the data deployment using a data deployment matrix and a data deployment graph.

2. Follow the previous question. Describe hardware and software components involved in accessing the database at the New Bedford headquarters from the Internet (e.g., for online flight reservations).

CHAPTER 10. DATA WAREHOUSE

10.1. Data Warehouse

In a large organization, it is unlikely to have just one database. Also, the database we have discussed thus far is normalized and is current. On the other hand, people need a variety of types of data which may not be normalized or may not be current. For example, if a student changes her name, the database keeps the new name, but where is the old name placed in the database for search?

A **Data warehouse** holds all kinds of data for supporting decision making activities. A data warehouse can be divided into **data marts**, and each data mart serves a particular functional division (e.g., finance, accounting, human resource management, etc.).

Unlike DMBS, data warehouse management systems are rather artistic. There is no matured system for data warehouse management.

10.2. Multidimensional Data and Data Cube

Dimensions are perspectives of data. For example, sales data can be viewed in the perspectives of time, location, type of product, sales team, etc. Technically, such dimensions are described by dimension tables, as explained later in this section.

Data warehouse typically deals with **multidimensional** data, called **data cube**, to describe facts of *what, who, where, how, when,* and/or *why.* For example, Sales can have three dimensions such as Product, Branch, and Time, as illustrated in Figure 10.1 as a 3D vision. Apparently, there is no way to illustrate hyper-space with more than 3 dimensions visually, but the concept of high-dimensional data for data warehouses is basically the same as the data cube in Figure 10.1.

The volume of data in data warehouse is usually large. You can imagine when the data set has a high dimensionality (e.g., 10 dimensions), and each dimension has a high number of levels (e.g., 100), the volume of data would be huge (e.g., 100^{10}). This would make it impossible to use an offline data cube for analytical processing.

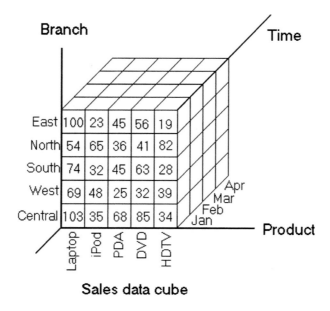

Figure 10.1. High-Dimensional Data and Data Cube

10.3. Creating Data Cube from Relational Database

The concept of data warehouse was developed in the 1990s during the information technology wave. For the time being, almost every data warehouse is built based on relational databases, although relational DBMS have been with us for longer than three decades. In a relational database, as we have learned, the unit of data for an entity is a two-dimensional table. In principle, any data cube can be represented by a set of normalized (i.e., without data redundancy) two-dimensional tables, and a data warehouse can then be represented by a set of data cubes. A typical method to present a data cube through two-dimensional data tables is **star schema**. Figure 10.2 shows an example of star schema for a data cube for sales.

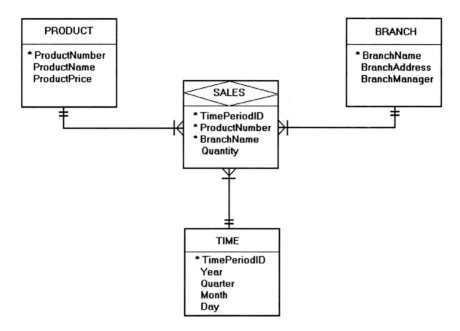

Figure 10.2. Star Schema for Generating High-dimensional Data Cube

As shown in Figure 10.2, the Sales data cube involves three dimensions: Product (*what*), Branch (*who*), and Time (*when*). The properties (i.e., attributes) and their data of each dimension are stored in a table. The values of the key of the table for each dimension represent the levels of this dimension. The **fact table** is the center of the star to represent the data cub. In this example, the SALES table keeps the sales data for the three-dimensional data cube. A relational DBMS (such as Oracle, DB2, and SQL Server) supports queries. A query can pull out needed data from each dimensional table to generate a data cube. For example, give a database modeled in Figure 10.2, the query *"Find all monthly sales which are generated by every branch for every existing product within the past four months"* will generate a sales data cube similar to Figure 10.1.

A data warehouse can have many fact tables. For instance, in addition to the SALES fact table, one can have an INVENTORY fact table.

Snowflake design is an extension of star schema design of multidimensional data for data warehouses. In the snowflake design, tables have 1:M relationships chains towards the fact table, the centre of the star schema. Figure 10.3 is an example of snowflake design which shows the shape of snowflake. Since the relationships between tables are always 1:M towards the fact table, the snowflake design makes it possible to generate meaningful very high dimensional data cubes.

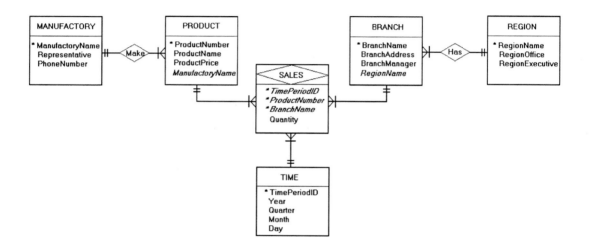

Figure 10.3. Snowflake Design

10.4. Definition of OLAP

OLAP (Online Analytical Processing) is one of the most popular **business intelligence** techniques in organizations. The word "**online**" means data availability. The volume of data for business intelligence is usually huge. To perform analytical processing, one must retrieve data from the data warehouse dynamically in the online fashion. A sophisticated OLAP tool makes the huge data warehouse **transparent** to the user, which means that the user is not aware of the location of data. After the data are downloaded to the user's PC side, an elementary analysis process is always offline. The phrase "analytical processing" means all activities involved in data analysis, including queries, statistical analysis, data visualization, and reporting. Thus, OLAP is a variety of data analysis techniques that are applied to very large data sets for organizations to discover interesting information.

10.5. Analytical Processing Tactics of OLAP

There are many tactics of OLAP data manipulation for discover useful information. Here we discuss major OLAP methods. People often use combinations of these methods for business intelligence.

A **query** is a set of instructions for processing the data with any dimensionality to extract useful information. One can create queries using SQL, or QBE (Query By Example) if the computation environment is end-user oriented (such as Microsoft Office). Using queries, one can find whatever needed data from databases though defining query criteria. Simple functions of queries include SELECT, SORT, GROUP, FILTER, etc. Sophisticated queries can provide information of the correlations among data (e.g., "*how many customers buy beer and diaper together*" in a well-known data mining story.)

Slicing is to reduce the dimensionality of data by fixing the level(s) of one or more dimensions to create **slices**. Figure 10.4 illustrates slicing.

Dicing is to divide the data cube into sub-cubes (called **dice**) for comparison, (e.g., "*actual vs. plan*", "*this year vs. last year*" etc.). Figure 10.5 shows dicing.

Sophisticated OLAP tools support slicing and dicing on online data warehouses. Apparently, working on offline data cubes using pivot tables, one can still perform slicing and dicing operations through manipulations of pivot tables.

Combinations of slicing and dicing with other methods, such as queries, statistical analysis, and data visualization, are also called **drill-down**, which means investigating information in increasing details.

Microsoft Excel is a useful tool for OLAP in the Windows environment. In fact, many OLAP software products use Microsoft Excel as the front interface with the user.

One of the important applications of databases and data warehouse in business is OLAP.

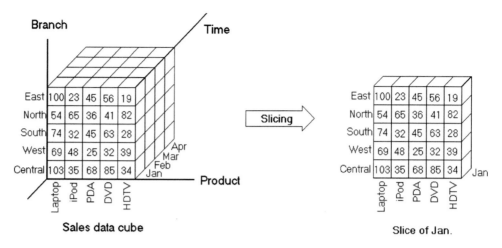

Figure 10.4. Slicing

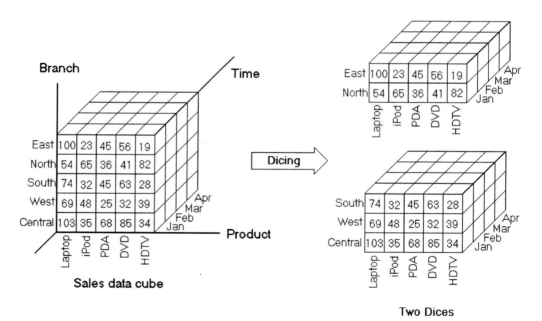

Figure 10.5. Dicing

10.6. Business Intelligence and Data Mining

Business intelligence is a broad category of applications and technologies of gathering, accessing, and analyzing a large amount of data for the organization to make effective business decisions. Typical business intelligence technologies include business rule modeling, data profiling, data warehousing and OLAP, and data mining. The central theme of business intelligence is to fully utilize massive data to help business gain competitive advantages.

In the information era the capability of analyzing and utilizing massive data lags far behind the capability of gathering and storing the data. New generation of computational techniques and tools are required to support information discovery in databases. This is the subject of **data mining**. Data mining is the process of trawling through data in the hope of identifying patterns of the data. Data mining is different from traditional data analysis in that it is aimed at finding unsuspected relationships which are of interest or value to the databases owners.

There is a well-known supermarket data mining story that consumers who purchase diaper are more likely to purchase beer at the same time in that supermarket. This story sounds interesting because such a purchase pattern is unsuspected. Apparently, these consumers may not be the typical ones. This story is an example to demonstrate to people how data mining could help the business to catch opportunities although such an unsuspected fact might be regional or short-lived. Clearly, data mining does not make good decisions automatically. In this story, the data mining result does not tell the supermarket manager whether beer and diaper should be placed together or far separately.

Due to the large number of dimensionality and the huge volume of data, traditional OLAP and statistical methods have their limitations in data mining. To meet the challenge of data mining, many artificial intelligence techniques such as neural networks, genetic algorithms, and other special data mining algorithms have been developed for data mining.

10.7. Data Resource for Organizational Knowledge Development

Data mining in data warehouse is a growing field in business. More often, information is used for decision making based on the data miner's prior or rational problem solving schema and creativity. Thus, the concept of data mining goes beyond the data and algorithms themselves, and data mining should be utilized to demystify the information discovery models and validate the information discovery results through human-computer collaboration.

Because of overlaps between business intelligence and knowledge development, many people do not fully understand the fundamental differences between business intelligence and knowledge management. Knowledge management is a set of practices of the creation, development, and application of human knowledge to enhance performance of the organization. Generally, knowledge management is concerned with human subjective knowledge flows, not data or objective information.

As the closing episode, we return the point about data, information, and knowledge we discussed in Chapter 1. There have been many myths and great confusion about the concepts of data, information, and knowledge these years. The true propositions are (a) databases organize structured data in the scientific way, and they are the foundation of data resources of the organization; (b) all structured data and unstructured data provide the data source for OLAP and data mining to generate interesting and useful information for the users; (c) the users learn from the instances of information and create knowledge which can be explicit or tacit, and the users can share and exchange their knowledge; (d) the users apply their existing knowledge to guide OLAP and data mining in order to obtain more information. This framework is depicted in Figure 10.6.

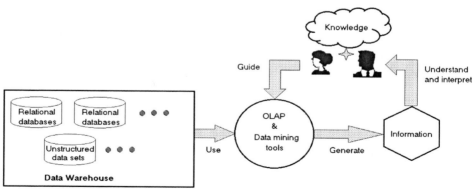

Figure 10.6. Data, Information, and Knowledge

Chapter 10 Exercises

1.* Recall the case of GreenHeating exercise question 2 of chapter 3. The GreenHeating database has the following tables that include a SERVICE-SPECS table for specifications of service activities.

HOUSE

*HouseAddress	HouseOwner	Insurance

HEATINGUNIT

*HeathingUnitID	UnitName	UnitType	Manufactory
	DateOfBuilt	Capacity	*HouseAddress*

TECHNICIAN

*EmployeeNumber	EmployeeName	Title	YearHired

SERVICE-SPECS

*ServiceSpecsID	ServiceSpecsName	ServiceDuration	RequiredFrequency

SERVICE

HeatingUnitID	*EmployeeNumber*	*ServiceSpecsID*	*Date*	*Time*

Design a multidimensional database using a star schema for a data warehouse for GreenHeating. The fact table will be SERVICE. Include snowflake features as appropriate.

2. Start Microsoft Access. Click on [Sample] on the left pane, you will see [Northwind 2007]. Click on it, you are now allowed to create the sample database called Northwind Traders on your PC. You may choose the folder you want to work on the sample database, and then click on button [Create]. You will see the following window.

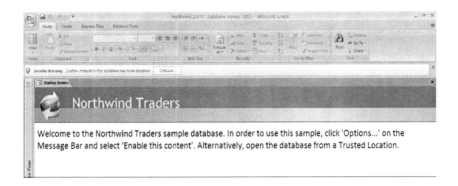

Click on [Option] and choose [Enable this content]. (Note that every time when you see Security Warning sign on the top of the window, you might need to take action.) Follow the instructions to open the Northwind Traders database, and review the queries and their datasheets.

Suppose you are the new CEO of Northwind Traders. You have an overview of the fictional data set, and understand the nature of the business of this company. Your assignment is to find interesting facts from the database using the OLAP and data mining concepts.

Minicase: *GreenJetNB (Chapter 10)*

Recall the GreenJetNB minicase in Chapter 3. GreenJetNB is a regional airline. It has several aircrafts and various commute itineraries between hubs and small cities. GreenJetNB's database keeps data of aircraft, pilots, past and future flights, passengers who traveled with GreenJetNB, aircraft maintenance work, and sales of airtickets. Design the following multidimensional databases using a star schema or snowflake design for a data warehouse.

a) The subject is "maintenance" that keeps track of maintenance records of aircrafts, operation pilots, maintenance jobs, and responsible maintenance companies over time periods.

b) The subject is "trip" that keeps track of the airfares and passengers' satisfaction ratings of trips over time periods.

TECHNICAL GUIDE I. AN EXAMPLE OF NORMALIZATION PROCEDURE

In this technical guide, we explain the normalization procedure through an example. In this example, we start with original datasheet samples, skip a trial ERD, and end up with the approved ERD. This example shows that it is possible, especially when the database is small, to carry out the logical database design without a trial ERD.

Step 1. Generate 0NF table

To design a database, one need to collect all of the business reports related to the data items which are supposed to be included into the computerized database. Any report containing original data samples could be rearranged in a two-dimensional table without missing values, called **relation** in relational database. Figure T1-1 shows how to arrange a sales report for a sales management system into a relation. Before the relation has its primary key, it is in unnormalized form or **0NF**.

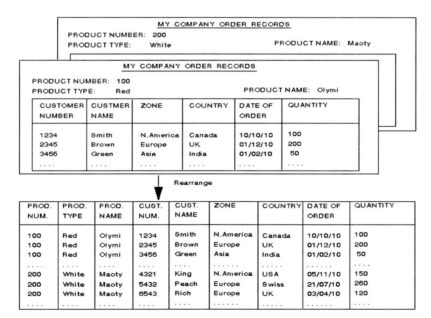

Figure T1-1. Generate Unnormalized Table (0NF) from Data Samples

Step 2. Establish primary key to generate 1NF tables

In the 0NF table, you make assumptions of functional dependencies based on "common sense" or the special situation of the system. As shown in Figure T1-2. If you know the value of [ProductNumber+CustomerNumber], then you can know the values of each attributes. Thus, [ProductNumber+CustomerNumber] is the primary key of this table, which becomes 1NF table.

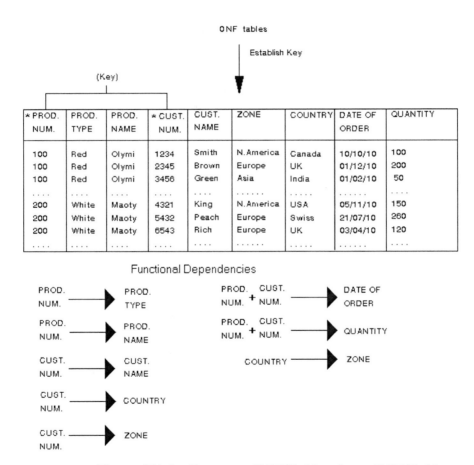

Figure T1-2. Generate 1NF Tables from 0NF Table

The 1NF relation has many problems. There is redundancy in the 1NF tables. For example, the same product names appear in several places.

Step 3. Remove partial key dependency to generate 2NF tables

To remove this **partial key dependency,** the 1NF table is decomposed into three 2NF tables, as shown in Figure T1-3.

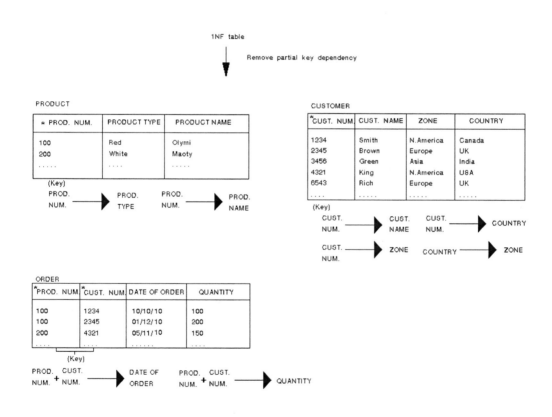

Figure T1-3. Generate 2NF Tables from 1NF Table

Step 4. Remove non-key dependency to generate 3NF tables

In the tables in 2NF, inspect non-key attributes to see if there is non-key dependency. In this example, Country is the determinant of Zone, and the two attributes are not keys. Thus, create a new table (AREA) with the two attributes, keep the determinant (Country) as the foreign key in the original table (CUSTOMER), and mark the determinant (Country) as the primary key of the new table.   Figure T1-4 shows the conversion results.

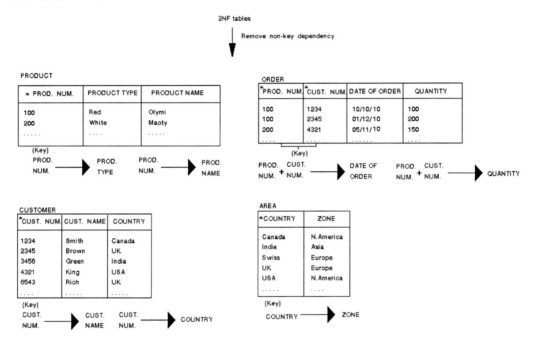

Figure T1-4. Generate 3NF Tables from 2NF Table

3NF is not a perfect normalised form; however, it is commonly considered a "good enough" form for database design, although there are higher-level normal forms.

Step 5. Reconciling all tables with common keys for the entire database

The analysis listed above is based on one application data sample; namely sales reporting. In an organization, there usually are many applications. A result of analysis of other applications related to the tables being analyzed should be combined if they have the same primary key. Generally speaking, the database designer needs to check over all applications and generate 3NF tables for the entire organization. For instance, suppose another set of data samples related to the PRODUCT table deals with price, and the firm wants to incorporate price information into the database. Then, the PRODUCT table would include attribute Price as shown in Figure T1-5. Clearly, such a reconciling must not violate 3NF.

PRODUCT

* PRODUCT NUMBER	PRODUCT TYPE	PRODUCT NAME	PRICE
100	Red	Olymi	100
200	White	Maoty	200
. . . .	. . . .	. . . . . .	. . . .

(Key)

Figure T1-5. Reconciling All Tables with Common Keys

Step 6. Draw ER diagram for the normalized tables

Once you obtain 3NF tables, you are ready to draw ERD for the database. Note that drawing ERD and performing normalization are interactive and iteration processes. Here, we start with data samples (data sheets) used in the business, then go through normalization, and finally draw the ERD for the database. You can use an alternative approach; that is, start with an ERD based on verbal descriptions of the business, then convert the ERD to tables and normalize the tables, and finally revise the ERD if needed. You feel free to use either approach.

The ERD of the above example is shown in Figure T1-6. Note the important features in our ERD format that can help you to avoid mistakes in building the

169

database.

(1) Any **M:M** relationship is converted into **1:M** relationships through an associative entity.

(2) Use detailed format for associative entities (e.g., *ORDER*), including combination keys (e.g., *CustomerNumber*, *ProductNumber*, and DateOfOrder).

(3) For each entity (including associative entity), mark the primary key with * clearly.

(4) For each **1:M** relationship (or the special case **1:1**), place the primary key in the **1**-side (e.g., Country in AREA) into the **M**-side as foreign key (e.g., *Country* in CUSTOMER), and use Italic font for foreign keys.

(5) An ERD may show a pure relationship between entities (e.g., Locate in this case) that has no explicit table in the database. Note that, in this ERD format, except for these pure relationships in the diamond shapes, any notation must have its corresponding representative item in the database.

Optional Step: Denormalization

For practical applications, denormalization is often useful for the efficiency of data access. Denormalization is an analysis procedure to build a certain amount of redundancy into the data base by combining normalized tables. Denormalization is acceptable as long as you do it for a good reason. For instance, let us consider the 2NF table CUSTOMER in Figure T1-3. From a practical point of view, this 2NF table might have no serious negative consequence if the relationship between CUSTOMER and AREA is not a major concern in the business other than the postal office or a delivery company. Obviously, the 2NF table have better information integration than the 3NF tables in this case. We can view this issue in another perspective. Suppose this company is not concerned with the functional dependency County → Zone. Then, the CUSTOMER table with Country and Zone is in 3NF.

This is the classic example of argument against "over-normalization" in the database area that it would be a good practice to place all data items for the address in the same table (e.g., [... StreetNumber, Street, City, State, ZipCode ...]) instead of establishing a separate table called ZIP[*ZipCode, City, State] for 3NF.

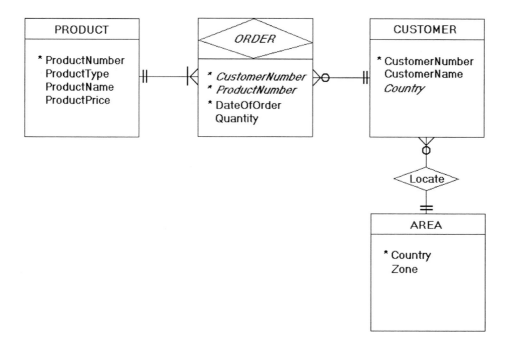

Figure T1-6. Approved ER Diagram for the Database with 3NF Tables

TECHNICAL GUIDE II. CONSTRUCTING A DATABASE USING MICROSOFT ACCESS

Typeset Convention

Bold - important term that has specific definition and concept

UPPERCASE - name of entity
UPPERCASE - name of relationship, or associative table, between two entities

`MonoSpace` - name of file, table, attribute, query, form, report, of the database etc.

> `tbl` – prefix of table name (e.g., `tblStudent`)
> `qry` – prefix of QBE query name (e.g., `qryStudent2012`)
> `sql` – prefix of SQL query name (e.g., `sqlStudentMIS`)
> `frm` – prefix of form name (e.g., `frmStudent`)
> `rpt` – prefix of report name (e.g., `rptStudent`)

> [**Note:** It is a good practice to use a single Camel Style word (without a space) for any name of table, attribute, query, form, and report; e.g., `StudentName`.]

* indicates the primary key

Lowercase indicates foreign key

`[Monospace]` – menu item or icon for clicking

The Example for Hands-On Practice

This technical guide provides detailed instructions to build a toy database that implements the following ERD.

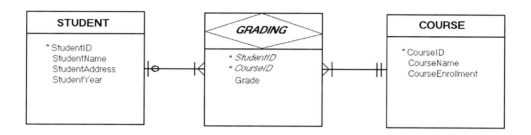

1. Overview of Microsoft Access DBMS

Microsoft Access is an end-user oriented DBMS, and has limited capacity. For instance, Microsoft Access provides no function for physical design of the database, and limited utilities for relationships of tables. Before we learn how Microsoft Access can be applied to create and use your own database, we give an overview of database construction and manipulation that available in the Microsoft Access environment.

1.1. Table

The first thing for database construction is to create tables using Microsoft Access. You are allowed to perform the following processing on table.

(1) Give a name to the table you are creating. For example, you can name `tblStudent` for the STUDENT entity. Here, we use common conventions: `tbl` means table.

(2) Define the attributes of the table. For example, you can create `StudentID`, `StudentName`, `StudentAddress`, `StudentYear` as the attributes of `tblStudent`.

(3) Declare the key of the table. For example, you are allowed to declare that `StudentID` is the key of table `tblStudent`. Key ensures unique record and makes the database manipulation efficient.

(4) Declare the data type for each attribute. For example, you may use **Text** for `StudentID`, `StudentName`, `StudentAddress`, and use **Number** for `StudentYear`.

(5) Display the table you created.

(6) Add records to the table.

(7) Delete records from the table.

1.2. Relationship

One of the major functions of relational DBMS is to define relationships between tables and maintain the data in accordance with these relationships. As we pointed out, Microsoft Access has limited utilities in defining relationships, but allows you to do many operations as described below.

(1) Create one-to-one relationship between two tables.

(2) Create one-to-many relationship between two tables. Many-to-many relationship must be convert to two one-to-many relationships using a junction (associative) table.

(3) Choose the option of enforce referential integrity.

(4) Choose the option of cascade update related attributes of the two tables.

(5) Choose the option of cascade delete related records of the two tables.

(6) Define join properties.

(7) Delete a relationship.

1.3. Query

The major purpose of database is to use the data stored in tables for particular process or decision making. A **query** is a function that retrieves data from the database. Using Access, you are allowed to create queries and other operations as described below.

(1) Create a query. For example, you may want to create a query that displays names of all students who are enrolled in the 2010 class. In this example, only `tblStudent` is

used for this query. You are allowed to create queries using **multiple tables**. For instance, you may want to create a query that displays names of all students who are enrolled in the 2010 class **and** have grade "A" in "MGT311". In this case, `tblStudent` and `tblGrading` must be used concurrently.

(2) Give a name to the query you created. For example, you may give `qryStudent2010` to the query that displays students in the 2010 class. Here, `qry` means query.

(3) Use the queries you created. You are allowed to click on the icon of query and retrieve the needed data from the database.

1.4. Form

Data of tables and queries can be displayed in different format. A **form** is used to display data from a table or query in a particular format on the screen. If you do not use forms, all data are displayed in a default format which is less user-friendly. In this sense, form is a secondary application of Microsoft Access. Major functions of Access for form are summarized below.

(1) Create and design a form. For example, you may want to create and design a form for table `tblStudent` to display the student data in a user-friendly way.

(2) Give a name to the form you created. For example, you may name `frmStudent` for the form that displays student data. Here, `frm` means form.

(3) Use the form you created. You are allowed to click on the icon of form and display the data in the designed from.

Switchboard is a special type of form that allows you to implement a user-computer interface for the database. We will further discuss on switchboard in the next section.

1.5. Report

Data of tables and queries can be printed on paper in different format. A **report** is used to print data from a table or query in a particular format to fit the size of the paper. You can also add logos and images to a report for printing. In this sense, report is also a secondary application of Access. Major functions of Access for report are summarized below.

(1) Create and design a report. For example, you may want to create and design a report for table `tblStudent` to print the student data in an organized format on paper.

(2) Give a name to the report you created. For example, you may give `rptStudent` to the report that prints student data. Here, `rpt` means report.

(3) Use the report you created. You are allowed to click on the icon of report and print the data on the printer.

There are other end-user oriented utilities in Microsoft Access for database construction and manipulation as you can learn from your project.

2. Hands-On of Microsoft Access: Step-by-Step Basics

This section provides basics of step-by-step hands-on of Microsoft Access 2007 for you to practice. Remember, in Microsoft Access one thing can be done in a variety of different ways. However, if you are confused in the middle of practice of this step-by-step hands-on, you'd better start over again from the point where you are lost. If you have difficulties in using Microsoft Access, please refer to section 2.13 of this technical guide to find possible solutions. Students are encouraged to further use Microsoft Access online help to learn more about Access for the database project.

2.1. Start Access and Prepare to Create a Database

Find Microsoft Access on your PC, depending on the installation setting, and load it (see Figure T2-1).

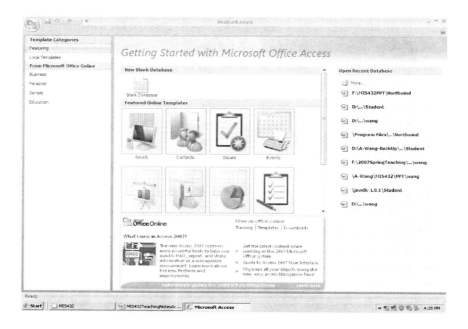

Figure T2-1. Load Microsoft Access 2007

Click on [Blank Database] icon. You will have [Blank Database] pane on the right side (see Figure T2-2). You are requested to choose the folder you want store your database, and type your database name (e.g., Student.accdb) for the new database. Next time you can click on the **Office Button** on the upper-left corner of the ribbon to open this database using this name. Note that, for the security purpose the Access environment often gives you **Security Warning** when you open an existing database. In such cases, you need to click on [Options] on the top [Security Warning] banner and click on [Enable this content].

At the point of the first time you use Access, you click on [Create] to create a new blank database.

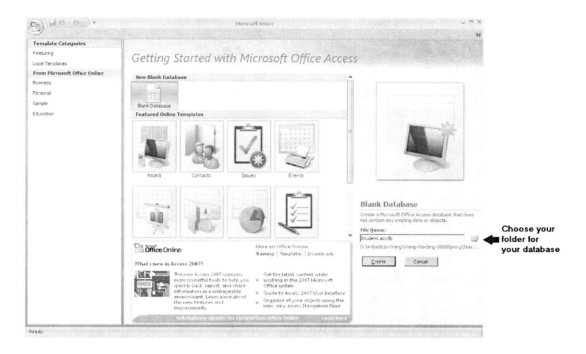

Figure T2-2. Create a New Database

Figure T2-3 shows the typical screen you will work on. On the upper-left corner, you can see an [Office Button] for [Open], [Save], [Print], etc. On the top, you can see top menu such as [Home], [Create], ... [Datasheet]. Click on a top menu item, you can see a **Ribbon** which contains a variety of commands for the menu item. The left side of the screen is the **Navigation Pane**.

In Figure T2-3 you can see the **Table Tools** and **Datasheet** ribbon, as well as the working pane for a table. Now it is ready to create a new table.

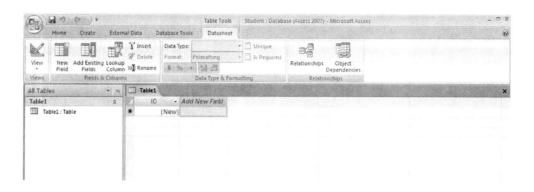

Figure T2-3. Table Tools Pane and Datasheet Ribbon

2.2. Create a New Table and Design It

On the **Datasheet Ribbon,** click on [View] icon and you will enter the **Design View**. You are requested to give a table name. In the [Save As] pane, you type the name for the table tblStudent (see Figure T2-4), and click on [OK]. You will see the design pane of the table (see Figure T2-5).

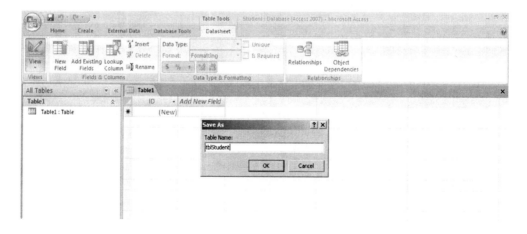

Figure T2-4. Enter the Design View to Design a Table

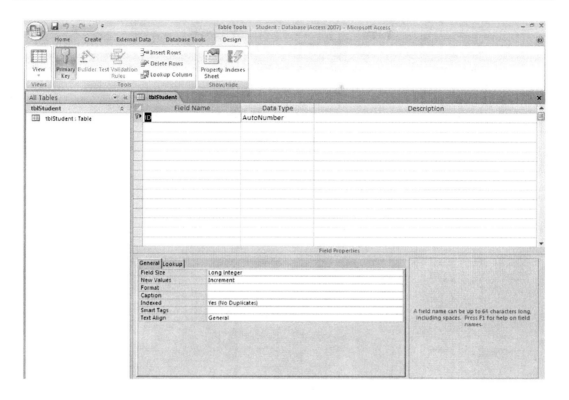

Figure T2-5. The Design View of the Table

You type StudentID for Attribute Name. To declare StudentID as the **primary key** if the system does not assign it automatically, highlight it and then click on [Primary Key] on the top menu. Note a small key icon marked on StudentID.

It is recommended to choose [Text] for the Data Type of keys, but not to use the default type AutoNumber. You design other attributes for the table as shown in Figure T2-6.

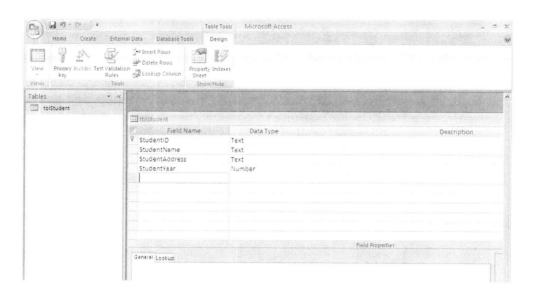

Figure T2-6. Design Table tblStudent

2.3. Create More Tables

On the top menu click on [Create] and then choose [Table] on the ribbon (see Figure T2-7). You will create another table (see Figure T2-8).

Figure T2-7. Use Ribbon to Create Another Table

Figure T2-8. Create a New Table

You crate the second table tblCourse with attributes CourseID, CourseName, CourseEnrol. Note that you need to use "Text" type for CourseID, and "Number" for CourseEnrol.

Similarly, you create the third table tblGrading with attributes StudentID, CourseID, Grade. Note that you need to declare a **combination key** for tblGrading, because the grade is functionally dependent on both StudentID and CourseID. To do so, in the design view you drag on and highlight both StudentID and CourseID, and click on the key icon on the ribbon, as shown in Figure T2-9. Note that each attribute of the combination key is a foreign key, and should have the same **domain of values** (the same data type) as its corresponding primary key.

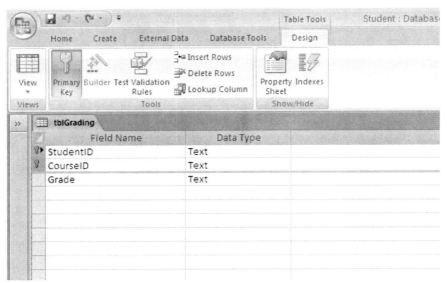

Figure T2-9. Declare Combination Key

2.4. Define Relationships between the Tables

Close all tables by right clicking the table tabs and then [Close]. Click on top menu [Database Tools] and [Relationships] icon, you will see **Relationship Tools** pane. You are now allowed to create relationships and edit relationships by yourself. On the top menu, click on [Design] and then the [Show Table] icon. You will see the **Show Table** pane (Figure T2-10). You choose tables needed for the relationships. If the relationships represented by connections are not shown up, click on the key attribute on one table and drag to the corresponding key of the other table as a **foreign key**. You will have a connection between the two tables. Right-click on the connection, and you will see the **Edit Relationships** pane and are allowed to define the relationship and its **referential integrity** rules (see Figure T2-11). Check the [Enforce Referential Integrity] checkbox in the Edit Relationships pane, and you will see that the "One-To-Many" type relationship has been created.

You are not allowed to change Relationship Types (1:1 or 1:M) in the relationship pane. To define a "one-to-one" type relationship instead of "one-to-many", you must go back to table design, find the foreign key which associates with the relationship, in its **Field Properties** pane define [Indexed] by choosing [Yes (No Duplicates)] for the 1:1 relationship.

Note that the relationship diagram displayed in Access is not really an E-R diagram, as the relationships are not shown as explicit as an E-R diagram.

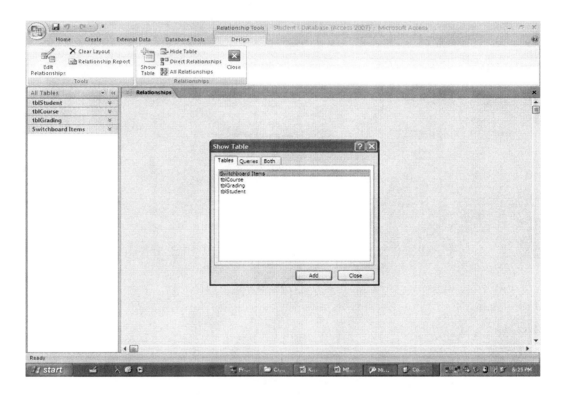

Figure T2-10. Relationship Tools and Show-Table Pane

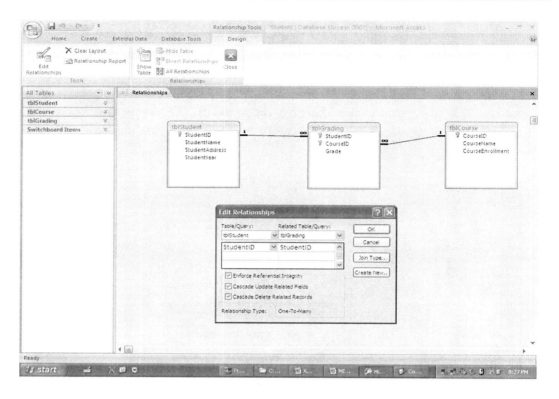

Figure T2-11. Edit the Relationships between Tables

For your database project, you need to check over all relationships before you can input data to all tables. Make sure the relationships implemented by the DBMS are identical with the approved ERD.

2.5. Input Data to a Table

You should never input data to tables before you complete the ERD, design all tables, define all relationships, and make sure all relationships are correct. Otherwise, your database might become a collection of garbage data.

To input data to a table, click on the [View] icon on the ribbon again and you enter the **Datasheet View**. You type the sample data. You check the datasheets of the three tables, as suggested in Figures T12, T13, and T14.

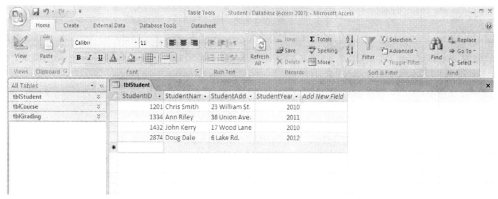

Figure T2-12. Datasheet of Table tblStudent

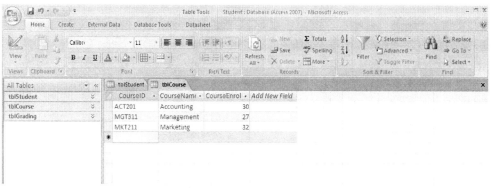

Figure T2-13. Datasheet of Table tblCourse

Figure T2-14. Datasheet of Table tblGrading

At this point of hands-on, you must pay attention on the sample data that do not violate data integrity. For instance, you must not input a grade in `tblGrading` for a student who does not exist in `tblStudent`. Similarly, you must not input a grade in `tblGrading` for a course which does not exist in `tblCourse`.

2.6. Create a Query for a Single Table Using QBE

Before you create queries, you must make sure all tables are normalized and all relationships are correctly defined, or you would have many problems with queries. In the MS Access environment, you can create queries by using either **Query Wizard**, or so called the **Query By Examples** (QBE) technique through **Query Design**, or **SQL**. Query Wizard is easy to use, and you can learn it by yourself. Query Wizard can implement simple queries. QBE and SQL can be used for more sophisticated queries. We discuss SQL later in this section. In this sub-section we learn QBE. QBE allow us to view tables, attributes, and relationships when you design queries.

Close the tables and relationships you have worked on. Click on [Create] on the top menu and click on [Query Design]. You will see the **Query Design** and **Show Table** pane (Figure T2-15). On the Show Table pane, click on the [Table] tab, and you will see a list of tables. You choose `tblStudent`, and click on the [Add] button. After you close the `Show Table` pane, you will have the design pane like Figure T2-16.

On the query design pane, click on the attributes you want to include in the query on the shown `tblStudent` table, say `StudentID`, `StudentName`, and `StudentYear`. In the lower pane, you are allowed to set **criteria** for the query. In this example, we want to see all students of the 2010 class, and type `=2010` in the `StudentYear` column in the criteria cell, as shown in Figure T2-17.

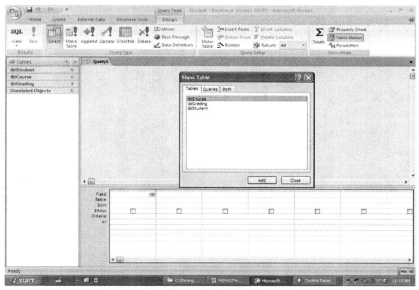

Figure T2-15. Design a Query

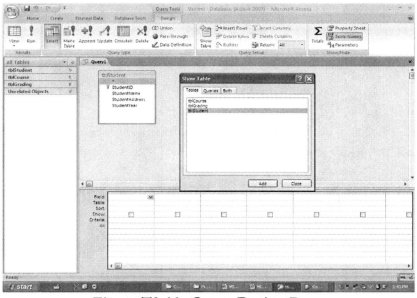

Figure T2-16. Query Design Pane

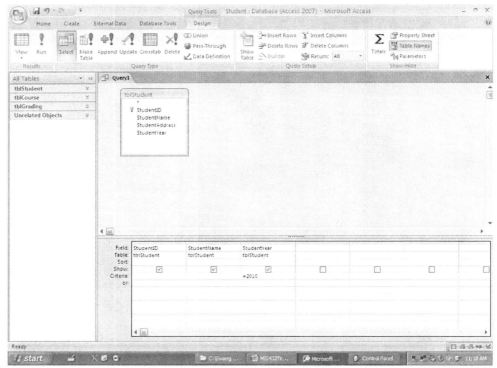

Figure T2-17. Design a Single-Table Query

Close the Query Design pane. You will be requested to give the name of the query you created. You type `qryStudent2010` for the name, and click on [OK] (see Figure T2-18). You click on the [Run] icon on the upper left corner of the ribbon, and will see the query result (see Figure T2-19).

You close the query design pane and quite the design mode. On the **Navigation Pane** (the left side of the screen), you can view and run the tables and queries you have created.

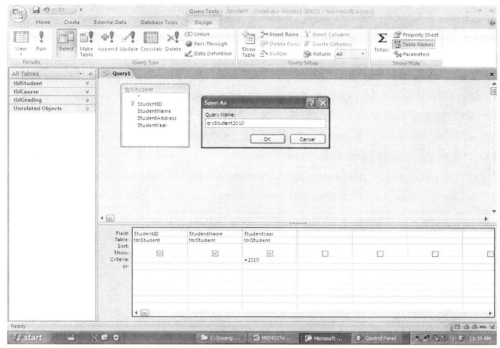

Figure T2-18. Save a Query

Figure T2-19. The Query Result of the Single-Table Query

2.7. Create a Query on Multiple Tables Using QBE

The procedure to create a query on multiple tables is not much different from that for a single-table query if you have defined the relationships of tables for your database. If you have defined the relationships between the involved tables correctly before creating a multiple-table query, the first thing you need to do is selecting more than one table when you work on `Show Table` pane (Figure T2-15). If the relationships between the tables have not been defined or defined incorrectly, queries on multiple tables often give unpredictable wrong results.

As an example, we choose `tblStudent` and `tblGrading`. Make sure that shown the relationship between the two tables is correct. Set the criteria for the query that is to find the students who receive "A" in MGT311, as shown in Figure T2-20 of the working `Query Design` pane. Figure T2-21 shows the query result.

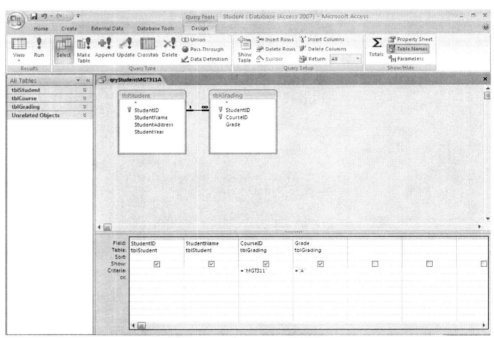

Figure T2-20.   Design a Multiple-Table Query

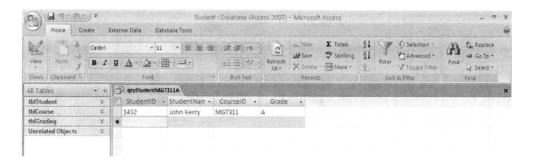

Figure T2-21. Query Result of the Multiple-Table Query

You can set contingent criteria for a query. For instance, if you set [Input Course ID] in the criteria of the CourseID attribute, the query will ask the user to input the value of CourseID depending on the user's needs. In the next section we will discuss SQL behind those queries.

2.8. SQL in Microsoft Access

2.8.1. View SQL of a query created by QBE in Access

Recall the query you have created, qryStudent2010 as shown Figure T2-18. Click on the query on the Navigation Pane, you can view the query result. Right-click on the query tab, and choose [SQL View] on the menu (see Figure T2-22), you can view the SQL code generated by the Access database management system when the qryStudent2010 was created (see Listing T2-1 and Figure T2-23).

```
SELECT  tblStudent.StudentID,
        tblStudent.StudentName,
        tblStudent.StudentYear
FROM    tblStudent
WHERE   (((tblStudent.StudentYear)=2010));
```

Listing T2-1. An Example SQL Code for Query

193

The SQL in Listing T2-1 means: select the data of `StudentID`, `StudentName`, and `StudentYear` from table `tblStudent` where `StudentYear` is equal to `2010`. We will describe SQL syntax later in this section.

Note: You may find that the style of SQL code generated by Access through QBE is little bit different from the normal style as shown in the textbook. For the course project, you need to write SQL by yourself as instructed in the next sub-section. Do not use QBE generated SQL code to substitute your own SQL for your project. Your SQL script is not supposed to be viewed in QBE; otherwise, QBE will change the style and will make it impossible to differentiate whether the SQL script is QBE generated or written by yourself.

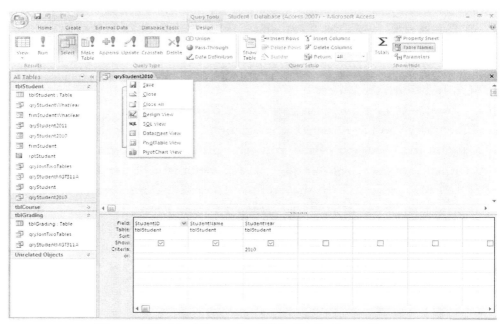

Figure T2-22. View the SQL Code for a Query

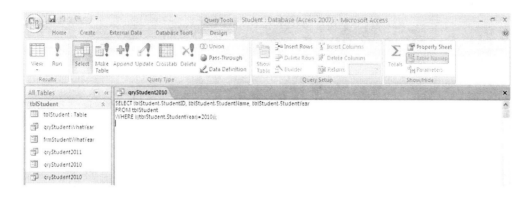

Figure T2-23. The SQL Code of qryStudent2010

2.8.2. Write and run SQL in Access

To edit SQL in Access,

- Open the database.
- Click on [Create] on the top menu, and choose [Query Design] in the ribbon.
- Close the Show Table pane.
- Right-click on the query tab and choose [SQL View]. Or, you can click on [SQL View] on the ribbon. Now you have the SQL edit window (similar to Figure T2-23 except for that it has word "SELECT;" only. and you are ready to write SQL code here.
- After editing SQL, you can save it as a query. To run the SQL, you click on the button marked with ! on the ribbon.

The SQL code in Listing T2-2 joins the two normalized tables tblStudent and tblGrading to show the denormalized data for users.

```
SELECT   tblStudent.StudentID, StudentName,
         CourseID, Grade
FROM     tblStudent, tblGrading
WHERE    tblStudent.StudentID = tblGrading.StudentID;
```

Listing T2-2. SQL of Joining Tables

It will display all students' number, names, the numbers of the courses they have taken, and their grades, as shown in Figure T2-24.   Note that, since the same attribute name `StudentID` are used in the two different tables, you must quote the table name to specify which table `StudentID` refers to.

Note: To learn SQL, you must write SQL queries without using QBE. Use [SQL View] (not [Design View]) for viewing and editing SQL scripts. If you modify QBE generated SQL code, Access always converts the modified SQL code back to the original style which indicates that the SQL code is not written by yourself. Also, for your course project, you need to use `sql` as the prefix for the name of queries, e.g., `sqlStudentGrades`, and test and run the SQL queries without contacting QBE.

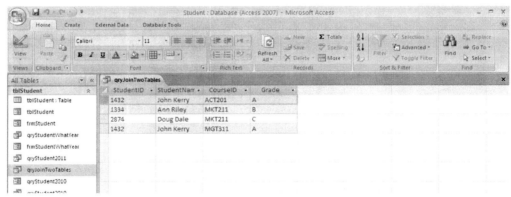

Figure T2-24. Execution Result of Joining Tables

2.9. Create a Form

Close all tables and queries you have worked on. As discussed earlier in this technical guide, Form and Report are secondary utilities of DBMS. Here we show how it is easy to use **Form Wizard**. Click on [Create]-[Form]-[More Forms]- [Form Wizard] on the ribbon, and you will see **Form Wizard** pane as shown in Figure T2-25.

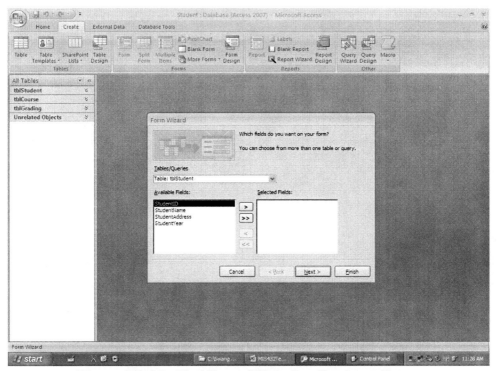

Figure T2-25. Use Form Wizard to Design a Form

On the Form Wizard pane, click on the [Tables/Queries] drop-down menu, you will see all tables and queries you have created. As an example, choose table tblStudent, select all attributes for the form, and click on [Next] button. You will have many steps that allow you to specify the form in a variety of formats.

You may try different options, and click on [Next] after every step. Finally, you click on the [Finish] button and give the name of the form, say, frmStudent. You return to Database pane, and can see the icon of the form. Click on the icon, and you will see the form (Figure T2-26). You can view and update tblStudent data from this form. Compare Figure T2-26 with Figure T2-7, and you can see that tblStudent and frmStudent are virtually the same, but the form is more user friendly to read and edit.

To further customize the generated forms, you right-click on the form tab and click on [Design View] on the menu, and you will be allowed to redesign the form. For learning more about graphical user interface, which is not a major topic in this database course, students are encouraged to embed images, buttons, and combo menus into forms.

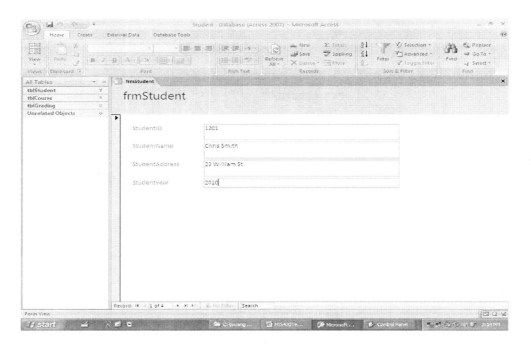

Figure T2-26. An Example of Form

2.10. Create a Report

The procedure to create a report is almost the same as the procedure for creating a form. The only difference between the two is that you click on [Create]-[Report Wizard]. As an example, we choose tblStudent as the base for the report. The wizard allows you to specify the report in a variety of formats. After several steps, you can view the report you created. It is similar, but may not be identical, to Figure T2-27 which has been polished through customization. To further customize the Wizard generated reports, you right-click on the report tab and select [Design View] on the menu, and you will be allowed to redesign the report. You can see that report allows you to print the data in a readable format on paper.

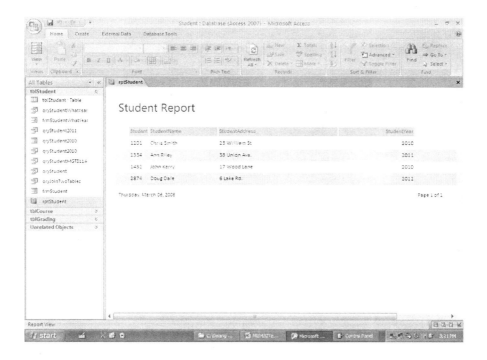

Figure T2-27. An Example of Report

2.11. Additional Features of the Microsoft Access Environment

The Microsoft Access is an independent end-user oriented database development environment, and possesses many utilities for design of the user-computer interface as well as business applications of the database.

The Navigation Pane on the left side of the screen can help you to organize your database contents including tables, queries, forms, reports, macros, etc. Choose [Object Type] (see Figure T2-28) to sort types of contents. You can also include [Search] in the Navigation Pane.

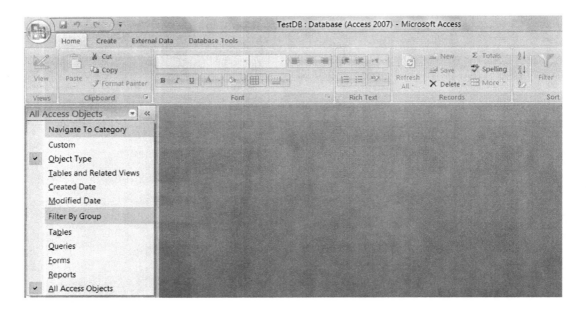

Figure T2-28. Navigation Pane

Microsoft Access provides many other utilities for database development. Students are encouraged to learn them through [Access Help (F1) 🔵] and other Microsoft Access professional manuals. One Microsoft Access official example called

`Northwind Traders` is an excellent example to learn. You can find it in `[Sample]` of when you open Access (Figure T2-1).

As a technical guide of the database textbook, this technical guide intends not to provide details of the instructions for secondary utilities of Microsoft Access. The authors believe that those technical skills are not essential for the database course at the present level but are important for students to learn on their own. Here, we summarize commonly used advanced features of Microsoft Access as follows.

(1) **Security** - You can include password protection for your database.

Figure T2-29. Password Protection

(2) **Switchboard** - You can have a well organized user-computer interface for the database through designing a switchboard form(s) that is applicable to the specific business application.

Click on `[Database Tools]- [Switchboard Manager]`. You can edit items for the switchboard. Figure T2-30 shows a simple switchboard created through **Switchboard Manager**. Note that, since Switchboard is a part of the user-database interface, Switchboard can only access forms (including other switchboards) and reports, but can't access tables and queries directly. Thus, you need to develop forms for any tables and queries that are linked to the switchboard. Figure T2-31 shows the three major panes that are used in `[Switchboard Manager]` for editing items for the switchboard.

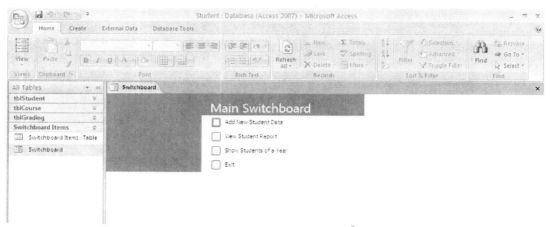

Figure T2-30. An Example of Switchboard

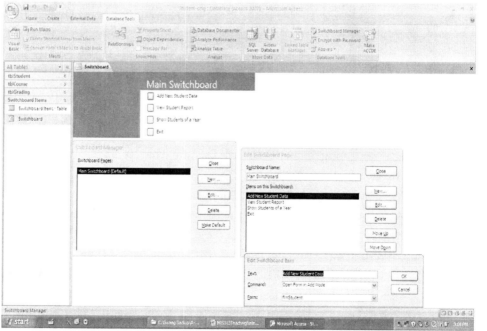

Figure T2-31. Three Major Panes Used for Editing the Switchboard

If you want to have sophisticated switchboard, you need to right-click on the switchboard tab and select [Design View] to design the switchboard.

Also, students are encouraged to develop multi-level and well-organized switchboards. For instance, you might want to have a top level switchboard to list all business areas for different types of users, and to have a second level switchboard for operations in each of these business areas, such as adding records and printing reports, and so on.

(3) **Macros** – Macros are programs/functions which can be executed repeatedly. There are two ways to create macros in Access. An easy way is to use [Create]– [Macro] to create macros without writing code. You may also use **Visual Basic for Applications** (**VBA**) (in [Database Tools]) to write code (or **Modules**) for relatively complicated business processes.

(4) **Startup** - The database can show a startup form with a logo through a macro named [AutoExec] or through the configuration of your database using the office button and then [Access Options] . You might also want to further develop macros and to design the command buttons on the startup form through its [Property Sheet] pane and then the [Event] pane so that the user can start the Switchboard from there. Figure T2-32 shows a simple example of startup form for the database.

In general, there are many different ways of design of user friendly user-computer interfaces. For this database course, design of user-computer interfaces is not a core component. In fact, a university academic course like this course might provide guides for students to develop technical skills, but is not supposed to train students with practical details. On the other hand, those technical skills are important for students to possess for their jobs in the future. Thus, students are encouraged to develop practical skills on their own through the course project.

Figure T2-32. An Example of Startup Logo

2.12. Data Dictionary

The final stage of a database project is to edit the **data dictionary** for the database. Microsoft Access can generate a data dictionary for the designer. Click on [Database Tools] on the ribbon and select [Database Documenter]. You will have the documenter pane (Figure T2-33). You can generate a database document here based on your needs (Figure T2-34), and meanwhile learn a variety of metadata for database management. To not over-document your data dictionary for your project report, you might have to edit a concise data dictionary based on your true understanding of computer generated documents.

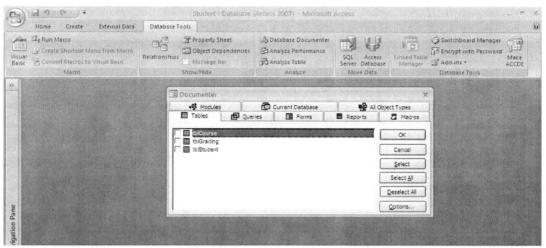

Figure T2-33. Database Documenter for Generating Database Documents

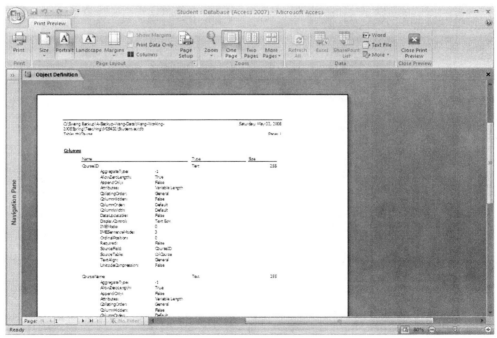

Figure T2-34. An Example of Database Document

2.13. Common Mistakes in Using Access and Possible Solutions

Access is an end-user oriented DBMS. It is easy to use. Nevertheless, beginners often make mistakes which Access can't fix by itself. The following table lists common mistakes and possible solutions.

Problem	Cause of the Problem	Solution
1. After open a database, Access does not response	Security protection	Click on [Options] on the top of [Security Warning], and set option to [Enable this content]
2. The key value of a table can't be changed	The default type of key values is set to AutoNumber	Change AutoNumber to Text
3. High digit 0 disappears in key value (e.g., 012 becomes 12)	The type of key values is set to Number	Change Number to Text
4. It does not allow to input data in table	The type of the values is set incorrectly; Or the data violate data integrity; Or the design of the table and the related tables is incorrect; Or the table is being used by other objects	Check the type of data. Check data consistency (e.g., do not try to input grade for a student who does not exist). Check the design of the table and related tables. CLOSE All tables, and reopen it
5. Being unable to set a combination primary key	You need to highlight the two or more attributes	Highlight the attributes of the combination key and then click on [Primary Key] button
6. It does not allow to change the design of a table when you are working on the table	You have already inputted data in the incorrectly designed table	Delete all data in the table before re-design. Or, CLOSE the table and delete it altogether and start a new table
7. It does not allow to switch to the Design View	Some objects are being used	CLOSE ALL tables, queries, forms, and reports that are being used
8. It does not allow to define relationships as desired in [Relationships Pane] (e.g., cannot show 1:M)	You have inputted data in the tables which have incorrect relationships, and/or the tables are open	Delete all data in the related tables, and redefine primary keys and relationships before inputting data, and CLOSE ALL tables
9. Query results are incorrect	The ER chart is incorrect, or the design of tables is incorrect	Check the ER chart, and then check the design of relevant tables and the relationships between the involved tables
10. The relationships type indicated in the relationships diagram is incorrect (e.g., it should be **1:1** instead of **1:M**, or *vice versa*)	The definition of the foreign key is set incorrectly	Go back to table design, find the foreign key which associates with the relationship, in its [Field Properties] pane, switch [Indexed] between [No Duplicates] and [Duplicates OK]
11. Previously successfully developed functions do not work this time	The contents might be disabled by the Security	Notice the security warning sign, click on [Option], and set [Enable]
12. Previous work has been lost	Wrong operations	Back up your work from time to time, and do not click on [Save] if you have made a wrong operation

3. Steps for Your Database Project

In conducting an Access database project, you need to follow the steps **strictly** as listed below in order to avoid generating a GIGO (garbage-in-garbage-out) database. To save time (trust me!), check each steps, do not skip steps, do not reverse steps, and do not mix steps.

☐ (1) Create a Learning-Test Zone (L-Zone) of Student Database which is exactly the same as the example in section 2 of this technical guide. Practice Access hands-on following section 2 step-by-step to fully understand the Access environment.

[**Note**: You'd better create a database that is exactly the same as the one in section 2 in this technical guide. You use this database for learning and test only. You must NOT use this hands-on database for your project. In other words, you must NOT mix L-Zone with your project (P-Zone). It would be a big mistake to use P-Zone as a hands-on tool for practicing Access because it would build-in errors in your project. Even during the development of your project, you might still want to return to the L-Zone to practice and learn new things without damaging the database of your project.]

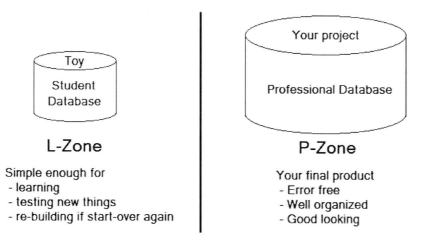

L-Zone

Simple enough for
- learning
- testing new things
- re-building if start-over again

P-Zone

Your final product
- Error free
- Well organized
- Good looking

☐ (2) Generate an idea of database for your project. Write a transcript for the business, or collect sample datasheets from the business. The transcript or the datasheets is a start point of your database design.

☐ (3) Develop ERD for your project. Define entities and associative entities. Define primary keys for the entities. Define cardinalities and modalities for the ERD. Pay attention to foreign keys and combination keys. Your ERD must be approved through normalization.

[*Note:* Before you finish your normalized tables and the relationships for your ERD, do not create a database for your project. Submit ERD to the instructor for approval before the next step.]

☐ (4) Create a Project Zone (P-Zone). Use Microsoft Access to create tables that implement everything defined in your ERD.

[*Note:* For 1:1 relationship, choose one of the two tables to include the foreign key. Make sure the 1:1 relationship is correctly implemented. For 1:M relationship, place a foreign key from the 1 side to the many side. For M:M relationship, you must create a table for the associative entity.]

☐ (5) Define the relationships for these tables in the Access environment (see subsection 2.4 of this technical guide). The relationships in Access and the approved ERD must be identical.

[*Note:* If you do not do this properly, you would have troubles in next steps. If your ERD is incorrect, or the relationship does not match the approved ERD, your database will be GIGO. Watch all 1:M linkages and check all primary keys and foreign keys (see Figure T2-11).]

☐ (6) Input sample data to each of the tables.

[**Note:** Do not input sample data until this step. Otherwise, you would have troubles in defining relationships between tables. When you input sample data, do not violate data integrity. For instance, do not try to input grade for a student who even does not exist in the student table.]

☐ (7) Develop queries for the database using QBE of the Access environment, and test them.

[**Note:** You need to write an English statement first to articulate the purpose of the query.]

☐ (8) Write SQL and test them.

[**Note:** You need to write an English statement first to articulate the purpose of the query. Remember, do not use modified QBE generated SQL code for this part – Access always changes modified QBE generated SQL code back to the strange style! Do not mix your SQL with QBE because your SQL code will be converted into QBE generated code.]

☐ (9) Develop forms (except for switchboard) for selected tables and queries.

☐ (10) Develop reports for selected tables and queries.

☐ (11) If you want to develop macros, you may do this now.

☐ (12) Develop switchboard and sub-switchboards that link all things together for your project. If you like, develop a start-up window.

☐ (13) Summarize the data dictionary for your database. Do not over-document the data dictionary.

☐ (14) Write up and organize your project report. Include the following items.
- Transcript or datasheets for the database to describe the business environment
- Approved ERD
- Meaningful Data Dictionary
- English descriptions of queries, along with your own SQL code and QBE generated SQL code for the queries
- Important screenshots especially your favorite parts of the project to remind the user to use.
- Reflection of what you have learned from this project.

☐ (15) Make a CD, or upload your whole package (report and the database artifact) to the instructor.

Suggested Time Frame for the Course Project

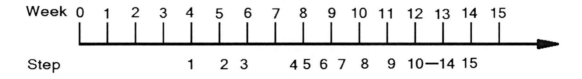

ANSWERS TO CLASS EXERCISE QUESTIONS AND REVIEWS

Chapter 1, Question 1.

Master data: Student profile records
Transaction data: Course registrations
Historical data: Financial aids
Secondary data: Transfer credits and courses
Subjective data: Advisors' comments

Chapter 2, Question 8.

a.

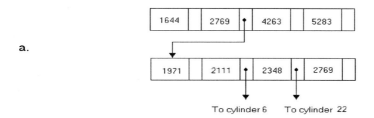

b.

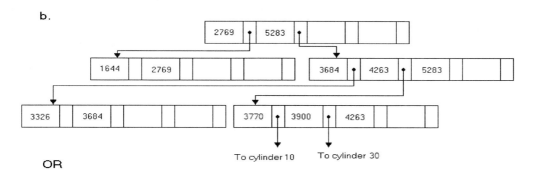

OR

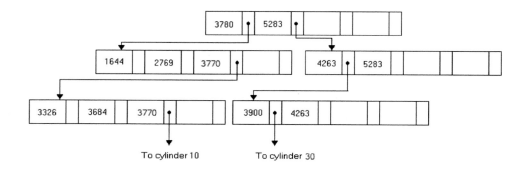

Chapter 3, Question 2.

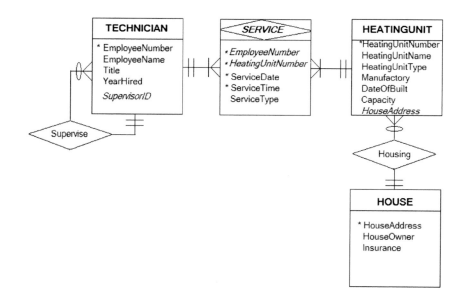

Chapter 4, Question 1.

Chapter 5, Question 3.

a. *BookTitle, FirstAuthor, Length*
3NF

b. *BookNumber, PublishDate, BookTitle, FirstAuthor*
2NF because of non-key dependency: BookTitle→FirstAuthor

*BookNumber, PublishDate, BookTitle
*BookTitle, FirstAuthor

c. [*BookNumber+*ClientNumber+*RentalDate], ReturnDate, RentalFee
3NF

d. *[*BookNumber+*ClientNumber+*RentalDate], ClientName, ReturnDate, RentalFee*

1NF because of partial key dependency: ClientNumber→ClientName

*ClientNumber, ClientName
[*BookNumber+*ClientNumber+*RentalDate], ReturnDate, RentalFee

e. *[*BookTitle+*ClientNumber], FirstAuthor, Length, ClientName, ClientAddress*

1NF because of partial key dependency: BookTitle→FirstAuthor

*BookTitle, FirstAuthor, Length
*ClientNumber, ClientName, ClientAddress
[*BookTitle+*ClientNumber] (This table indicates who rents this book. Note that the table in question follows the business rule that "The combination [BookTile+ClientNumber] is unique".)

Chapter 5, Question 4.

a) **Order ID, Order Date, Shipping Date, Customer ID, Customer Name, Customer Address*

2NF because of non-key dependency: CustomerID → CustomerName, CustomerAddress

Decompose it into 3NF tables:

*OrderID, OrderDate, ShippingDate, CustomerID
*CustomerID, CustomerName, CustomerAddress

b) *[*OrderID+*ProductID+*CustomerID], Customer.Address,
ProductName, ProductSalePrice, OrderQuantity*

1NF because of partial independency: CustomerID → CustomerName ….

Decompose it into 3NF tables:

*OrderID, Customer ID
[*Order ID+*Product ID], ProductSalePrice, OrderQuantity
*ProductID, ProductName
*CustomerID, CustomerAddress

(Note that one may have [*ProductID+*CustomerID] as a component of the original key. This table would meaningful for "who bought what". However, the business rule here is the combination [*ProductID+*CustomerID] is unique which may or may not be true.)

Chapter 6, Question 1.

a) *Find the owner of the house "285 Westport Rd".*

```
SELECT HouseOwner
FROM HOUSE
WHERE HouseAddress='285 Westport Rd';
```

b) *List the heating unit names and numbers of the Gas heating units which was built in house "285 Westport Rd".*

```
SELECT HeatingUnitID, HeatingUnitName
FROM HEATINGUNIT
WHERE UnitType='Gas'
AND HouseAddress='285 Westport Rd';
```

c) *List the heating unit number, date of built, manufactory, and all types of Gas, Electric, and Solar with capacity between 3000 and 4000 cub-feet from largest to smallest.*

```
SELECT HeatingUnitID, DateOfBuilt, Manufactory, UnitType
FROM HEATINGUNIT
WHERE UnitType IN ('Gas', 'Electric', 'Solar')
AND Capacity BETWEEN 3000 AND 4000
ORDER BY Capacity DESC;
```

d) *List the names of technicians who maintained a heating unit in "285 Westport Rd" along with the service type performed.*

```
SELECT EmployeeName, ServiceType
FROM TECHNICIAN, SERVICE, HEATINGUNIT
WHERE TECHNICIAN.EmployeeNumber=SERVICE.EmployeeNumber
AND HEATINGUNIT.HeatingUnitID=SERVICE.HeatingUnitID
AND HEATINGUNIT.HouseAddress='285 Westport Rd';
```

e) **Find the name and number of the largest Gas heating unit.**

```
SELECT HeatingUnitID, UnitName
FROM HEATINGUNIT
WHERE UnitType='Gas'
AND Capacity=
     (SELECT MAX(Capacity)
             FROM HEATINGUNIT
             WHERE UnitType='Gas');
```

Chapter 7, Question 1.

a) *There is a critical need to quickly list the heating units with a particular type.*

Build an <u>index</u> over the <u>UnitType</u> attribute of the <u>HEATINGUNIT</u> relation.

b) *There is a frequent need to list all heating unit numbers along with their unit types and houses.*

Make <u>vertical partition</u> of <u>HeatingUnitID</u>, <u>UnitType,</u> and <u>HouseAddress</u> in the <u>HEATINGUNIT</u> relation and separate them out physically.

c) *There is a frequent need to retrieve detailed data about a heating unit together with detailed data about the house in which it locates.*

One option is to use the <u>clustering</u> technique to bring <u>HEATINGUNIT</u> and <u>HOUSE</u> physically near each other on the disk.
Another option is to <u>merge </u>(denormalization) the <u>HEATINGUNIT</u> and <u>HOUSE</u> tables.

d) *There is a much more frequent and high priority need to access the records for Gas heating units than for the other types.*

Make <u>horizontal partition </u>of the <u>records with Gas type</u> in the <u>HEATINGUNIT</u> relation and separate them out physically.

e) *Due to large numbers of access activity, the HEATINGUNIT relation has become a bottleneck.*

<u>Duplicating</u> the <u>HEATINGUNIT </u>relation to route different queries to the different copies.

Chapter 10, Question 1.

The question does not specify what dimension you need to include in the design. One common assumption is to include the time dimension (*when*).

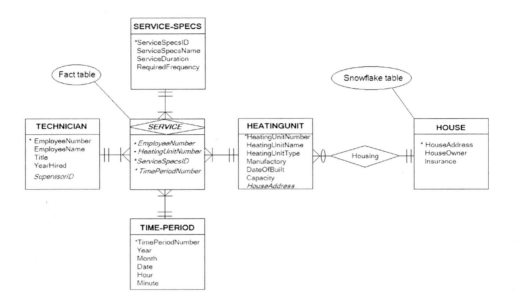

Review of Key Points of Problem Solving for Each Chapter

(Key points of Chapter 1 are incorporated with other chapters.)

Chapter 2: File organizations
> ? Important concepts of sequential file, random file, and indexed file organizations

Chapter 2: B-tree
> ♦ Given the number of index-pointer pairs for each index record
> ♦ Given the maximum key values on cylinders
> ? Construct a B-tree
> ? B-tree maintenance (index record splitting) in response to an overfull cylinder

Chapter 3: Constructing ER diagram
> ♦ Given a transcript or sample datasheets
> ? Draw an ER diagram to map each sentence given in the transcript
> or every data item in the datasheets
> ? Primary keys
> ? Foreign keys
> ? Cardinality, modality
> ? Binary, unary, ternary
> ? For M:M relationship, define associative entity and intersection data, and convert the M:M relationship into 1:M relationships (using physical ERD).

Chapter 4: Converting ER diagram to tables
> ♦ Consider the ER diagram you crated in U1-P2
> ? Convert the ER diagram you created in U1-P2 to relational database tables
> ? Mark CK, AK, PK, FK on each table based on common sense assumptions
> ? Define constraints for cardinalities and modalities

Chapter 4: Data retrieval and joining tables
Chapter 1: Data redundancy and integration

- ◆ Given tables of relational database
- ? Identify FK for implementing 1:M relationship
- ◆ Consider a data retrieval situation
- ? Steps of data retrieval (must be specific on the particular data)
- ◆ Consider a situation of merge of two tables
- ? Merge tables, and discuss redundancy and integration
  - • You may want to show the merged table to discuss specifically. Pay attention on the way of merging tables
  - ? Data modification anomaly

Chapter 4: Referential integrity

- ◆ Given tables and deletion rules (restrict, cascade, set-to-null)
- ◆ Given independent situations of record deletion
- ? What will happen for each of the situations

Chapter 5: Normalization

- ◆ Given a table with its attributes and their functional dependencies
- ? Determine 1NF, 2NF, or 3NF for the table
- ? Explain why the table is 1NF, 2NF, or 3NF
- ? If the table is not 3NF, normalize it into 3NF tables
- ? Concepts of BCNF and 4NF

Chapter 6: SQL

- ◆ Given the relational database 3NF tables
- ◆ Given English descriptions of queries
- ? Write SQL for each query
  - • CREATE, DROP, INSERT, UPDATE, DELETE commands
  - • SELECT command

- Major clauses
  (WHERE, GROUP BY, etc.) and operators (AND, OR, etc.)
- Pay attention on join (not explicit inner join/outer join format)
- Subquery (especially, for the uncertain criteria in the WHERE clause)

Chapter 7: Physical database design

♦ Given 3NF tables of a relational database

♦ Given independent situations

? State a technique of physical database design to improve the performance for each situation (use the following key words and specify the techniques)

- Adding index (*on what attributes*)
- Cluster files (*of what tables*)
- Denormalization – merge tables (*what tables*)
- Horizontal partitioning (*what table based on what criteria*)
- Vertical partitioning (*what part of what table*)
- Duplication (*of what table*)
- Add subschema (*what tables for the subschema, and for who*)
- New primary key (*what new key to replace what old key*)
- Substitute foreign key (*what new foreign key for which old one*)
- Store information/processed data (*what information*)

Chapter 8: Data dictionary

♦ Given the relational database 3NF tables

? Write a simple data dictionary for tables and attributes

Chapters 8: Database backup and recovery

♦ Given the relational database

? Describe a re-do or un-do backup and recovery strategy for the database

Chapter 9: Database on networks

◆ Given the relational database

◆ Given situations

? Design distributed database to fit all of the situations

• Explain the deployment of each table about
placement, partitioning (H. P. or V.P.), replication,
and/or combinations of these methods using
a data deployment matrix or a data deployment graph

Chapter 10: Star schema

◆ Given the relational database, and a need for the time dimension
for data warehouse

? Design star schema for a data warehouse

• Draw an ER diagram for star schema similar to Figure 10.2

INDEX

POWERPOINT SLIDES

Preface: Context of database design and implementation Preface-1	**Importance of Database** • Database is a key component of information systems - No database, no information system • Data is a valuable resource of the organization • Data resource management is a key part of business Preface-2
Database Design vs. **Business Process Design** • Database design is parallel with business process design for the information system development • Data modeling is parallel with process modeling for systems analysis and design • In this course of database, business process is not a focal point, but the generalized abstraction of data and their relationships is a focal point Preface-3	**Database Design vs.** **Business process Design (cont'd)** • It is assumed that students in this course have taken, or are taking concurrently, a prerequisite course on process modeling for business systems analysis and design • The central point of database design is that the database for the organization should support all types of business processes in the organization Preface-4
Reality of database • Historically, there are several types of database models, as we discussed later in the course • Information technology is the fast innovative field. Ironically, after it was introduced in the late 1970s and the early 1980s, the relational database model is still "the only" database model practically used in the IT industry • It is unlikely that the relational database model will be replaced by someone any soon Preface-5	**Unique features of This Textbook** • A good balance between core components and secondary components • A good balance between core knowledge and practical skill • A huge amount of material in the database area is boiled down to a manageable volume – "no waste moisture" • A built-in comprehensive study guide: appendices, answers to selected questions, reviews for tests, and PPT • Please use the textbook fully Preface-6

Chapter 1. Introduction

Ch1-1

Data Are Resource of the Organization

Data are valuable assets of the organization.

There are many types of data:

- Master data (e.g., customers)
- Transaction data (e.g., sales)
- Historical data (e.g., credit history)
- Secondary data (e.g., industrial average)
- Subjective data (e.g., marketing survey)

Ch1-2

Data, Information, Knowledge

- Data are raw facts
  For example (poll students)

- Information is a product of processed data
  For example (poll students)

- Knowledge is human interpretation of the real world
  For example (poll students)

Ch1-3

Database is about data, NOT about information, or knowledge

- Database discussed in this course emphasizes on data, not much on information and knowledge.
- Data warehouse, knowledge base.... are built on databases and more or less deal with information and knowledge

Ch1-4

Data Redundancy

- The central issue of database is data redundancy control
- **Data redundancy** occurs when the same fact is stored in more than one place

Ch1-5

Discussion on data redundancy

CUSTOMER- PURCHASE

CustomerNumber	CustomerName	CustomerAddress	CustomerPhone	Purchase	PurchaseTime
123456	Smith	Westport Rd.	588999	$200	10/20/2010 09:45am
234562	Green	Eastport Ave	509343	$300	10/23/2010 01:32pm
123456	Smith	Westport Rd.	500999	$150	11/08/2010 05:04pm

(a) Data redundancy occurs

Ch1-6

Discussion on data redundancy (cont'd)

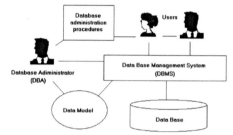

CUSTOMER

CustomerNumber	CustomerName	Customer Address	CustomerPhone
123456	Smith	Westport Rd.	508999
234562	Green	Eastport Ave.	509343

PURCHASE

CustomerNumber	Purchase	PurchaseTime
123456	$200	10/20/2010 09:45am
234562	$300	10/23/2010 01:32pm
123456	$150	11/08/2010 05:04pm

(b) There is no data redundancy if the data are stored in this way

Ch1-7

Database and Database Systems

- Objectives of database system:

- Controlled data redundancy
- Data consistency
- Data sharing
- Facilitate application development
- Wide-ranging data management functions

Ch1-8

Database System

Database administration procedures

Users

Database Adiministrator (DBA)

Data Base Management System (DBMS)

Data Model

Data Base

Ch1-9

Database Management System (DMBS)

- DBMS is software that manages the database:
- Support database construction and data access
- Control data redundancy
- Provide data integration
- Maintain data independency
- Monitor and improve data retrieval performance
- Control data security
- Enforce business rules and maintain data integrity
- Manage concurrency control
- Perform backup and recovery
- Maintain data dictionary
- Facilitate restructuring database

Ch1-10

Commonly used DBMS for relational database

- (1) ORACLE is Oracle Corporation's product.
- (2) IBM DB2 (or DB2) is IBM's product.
- (3) MySQL is a popular choice of database for use in Web applications, because it is closely tied to the popularity of PHP, an open-source server-side programming language.
- (4) Microsoft SQL Server was Microsoft's entry to the enterprise-level database market, competing against ORACLE and IBM DB2 in about 1989.
- (5) Microsoft Access was released in 1992 as an end-user oriented DBMS in the Microsoft Office suite. It does not support many sophisticated database management functions.

Ch1-11

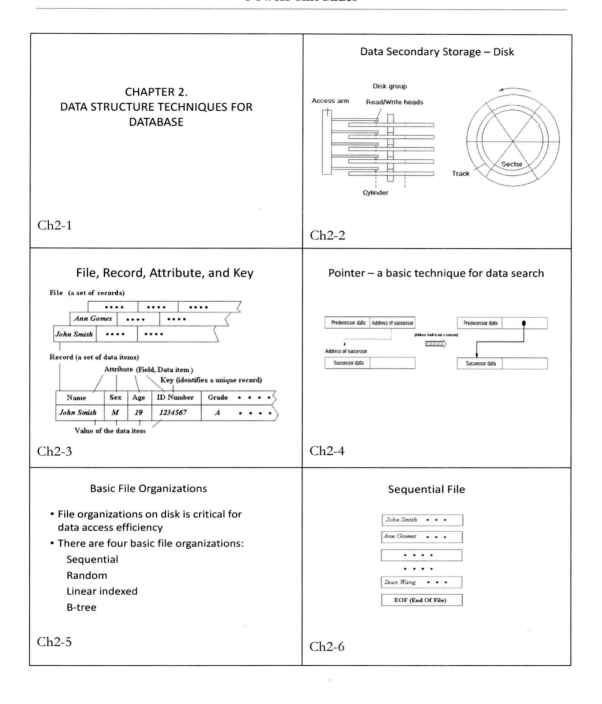

CHAPTER 2.
DATA STRUCTURE TECHNIQUES FOR DATABASE

Ch2-1

Data Secondary Storage – Disk

Ch2-2

File, Record, Attribute, and Key

Ch2-3

Pointer – a basic technique for data search

Ch2-4

Basic File Organizations

• File organizations on disk is critical for data access efficiency
• There are four basic file organizations:
    Sequential
    Random
    Linear indexed
    B-tree

Ch2-5

Sequential File

Ch2-6

Pros/Cons of Sequential Files

- Advantages of sequential files:
- (1) Saves space.
- (2) No record key is required.
- (3) Efficient when all of the records are sequentially processed (e.g. payroll processing).
-
- Disadvantages of sequential files:
- (1) It would take a long time to find a particular record.
- (2) It is difficult to update. For example, it is difficult to insert a record.

Ch2-7

Random Files

- Hashing function

Ch2-8

Pros/Cons of Random Files

- Random files are not common in modern databases
- Advantages of random files:
- (1) It can access an individual record very fast.
- (2) It is efficient in updating (e.g., adding and modifying records).
-
- Disadvantages of random files:
- (1) Sequential access is impossible.
- (2) A record key is necessary.
- (3) Wastes spaces.
- (4) Synonyms make the process slower.

Ch2-9

(Linear) Indexed File

Index Table

Record Key	Address of Record
3081	1010
4123	0239
1056	4320
. . . .	. . . .

DISK

1010 | 3081 | ABCD
4320 | 1056 | EDTY
0239 | 4123 | XDYH

Ch2-10

Pros/Cons of Linear Indexed Files

- Advantages of indexed files:
- (1) It can be used in both sequential and random access. Processing speed is fairly good for both.
- (2) It is efficient in adding a record, sorting and updating the file, if the indexed file is not huge.
-
- Disadvantages of indexed files:
- (1) A record key is necessary.
- (2) If the data file is huge, then the linear index table becomes a sequential disk file, and processing will be slow.

Ch2-11

B-Tree

- B-tree is the major file organization used in modern databases
- You need to understand the B-tree makes databases so powerful in data search
- You need to understand how the computer constructs B-trees and maintains B-trees
- After this chapter, you may not return to hands-on questions of B-tree, but you need to keep B-tree in your mind

Ch2-12

B-Tree

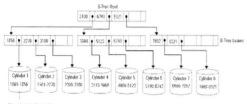

Ch2-13

B-Tree:
Find record with key value of 6000

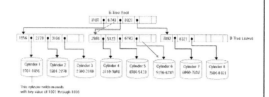

Ch2-14

Rules in B-Tree

- (1) A B-tree consists of index records that are organized into its tree. The tree has its root with one and just one index record on the top, and a number of levels.
- (2) Each index record accommodates the same number of pairs (4 in the example of Figure 2.7), and each pair can hold a key-value and a pointer.
- (3) Each index record is at least half full (in the example of Figure 2.7, at least 2 pairs in an index record are occupied with key-values and pointers, and the rest pairs can be empty).
- (4) In each occupied key-value-pointer pair, the pointer points to an index record at the next level or a disk cylinder, and the key-value is the maximum key value in the pointed index record or the maximum key value on the cylinder.

Ch2-15

B-Tree Maintenance
Cylinder 6 is full and add Cylinder 9

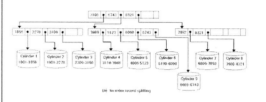

Ch2-16

B-Tree:
Splitting index records

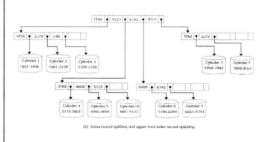

Ch2-17

Summary of B-Tree

- In our examples, B-tree is used for indexing key values. Actually, B-tree can also be used for non-keys.
- A database management system can construct and maintain a huge amount of B-trees so that random data access would be efficient.
- On the other hand, significant computational resource is devoted to B-tree construction and maintenance.

Ch2-18

Chapter 3.
Data Models

Ch3-1

Data Models

- A data model is a representation of complex data structures of the target real world, or system (e.g., Student Information System), for database design.
- There are four data models in the DB field:
  - Hierarchical model for hierarchical databases;
  - Network model for network databases;
  - Entity-relationship (ER) model for relational databases; and
  - Object-oriented model for object-oriented databases.

Ch3-2

ER Model: Entity

- Entity – a class of objects
  - Physiomorphic entity is a physically existing object; e.g., customer, student, and inventory.
  - Event entity represents an event of routine operations; e.g., game and credit approval.
  - Document entity is an artificial abstraction; e.g., degree.

Ch3-3

Entity – E.g., STUDENT

- Attributes – describe the entity, e.g., StudentID, StudentName ....
- Data type – each attribute has its data type, e.g., text, number...
- Instance – a value of attribute, e.g., John Smith
- Primary key – unique identifier of the entity, e.g., StudentID

Ch3-4

Entity

STUDENT
* StudentID
StudentName
StudentAddress
StudentYear

Ch3-5

ER Model: Relationship

- Relationship – Association between entities
  - Binary
  - Unary
  - Ternary
- Cardinality - Maximum number of instances of entities involved in the relationship
- Modality - Minimum number of instances of entities involved in the relationship

Ch3-6

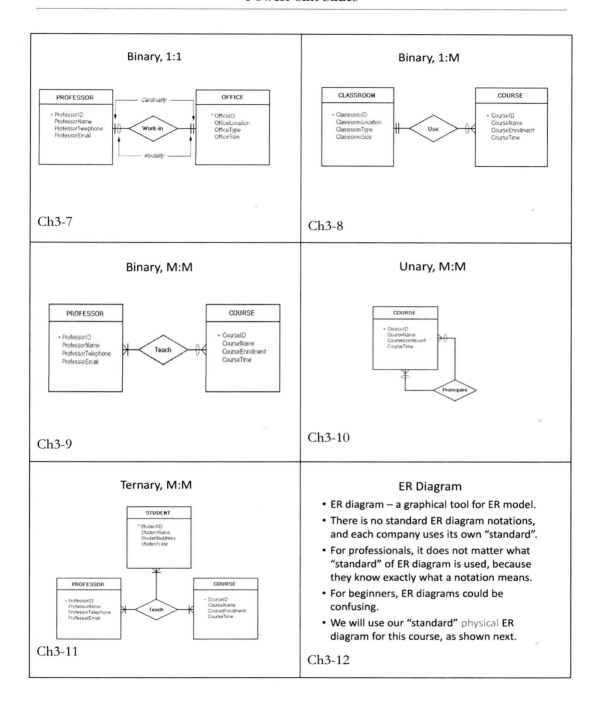

Binary, 1:1

Ch3-7

Binary, 1:M

Ch3-8

Binary, M:M

Ch3-9

Unary, M:M

Ch3-10

Ternary, M:M

Ch3-11

ER Diagram

- ER diagram – a graphical tool for ER model.
- There is no standard ER diagram notations, and each company uses its own "standard".
- For professionals, it does not matter what "standard" of ER diagram is used, because they know exactly what a notation means.
- For beginners, ER diagrams could be confusing.
- We will use our "standard" physical ER diagram for this course, as shown next.

Ch3-12

ER Model

- (1) The relationships between the instances of entities along with the cardinalities and modalities are not given, but are modeled by the database designer using ER diagrams. They depend on the **business rules** of the business environment, or the **assumptions** made for the particular database.
- (2) The cardinalities and modalities will be used by the database management system to enforce the pertinent business rules.
- (3) In relational database, there is no way to present M:M relationships directly in the database. Any M:M relationship must be converted into 1:M relationships through the use of **associative entity**, as discussed in detail later in this chapter.

Ch3-13

Instrument for Implementing 1:1 and 1:M Relationships – Foreign Key

- For a 1:1 relationship, you can arbitrarily choose the primary key from either entity and place it as the foreign key to the other entity However, if one of the modalities is 0, it is better to place the foreign key into the entity with the 0 modality
- For a 1:M relationship, you place the primary key of the entity with the 1 cardinality into the entity with the M cardinality as the foreign key.
- Foreign key in a table and its corresponding primary key in another table have the same domain of values (e.g., both have 7 characters)

Ch3-14

Foreign Key for 1:1

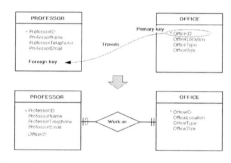

Ch3-15

Foreign key for 1:M

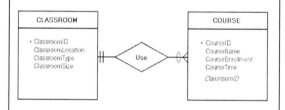

Ch3-16

Foreign key in unary 1:M

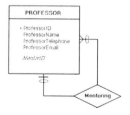

Ch3-17

Instrument for Implementing M:M Relationships – Associative Entity

- Foreign key only is incapable to implement an M:M relationship
- The associative entity converts the M:M relationship into two 1:M relationships which can then be represented in the relational database.

Ch3-18

Associative entity for implementing M:M relationship

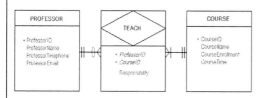

Ch3-19

Rules of Associative Entity

- (1) Once an associative entity is introduced, the M:M relationship becomes two 1:M relationships, and the associative entity is on the M sides between the two original entities. The original M:M relationship disappears.

- (2) To distinct an associative entity from an ordinary entity, a diamond symbol is used.

Ch3-20

Rules of Associative Entity (cont'd)

- (3) Follow the same rules of implementing 1:M relationships, place the primary key of the entity on the 1 side into the associative entity as the foreign key.

- (4) Usually, the combination of the foreign keys in the associative entity is the primary key of the associative entity.

- (5) An associative entity usually has its unique attribute(s) that is not a part of either of the original entity but describes the characteristics of the associative entity, called **intersection data**.

Ch3-21

Associative entity in unary

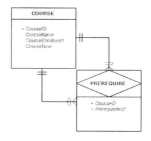

Ch3-22

Associative entity in ternary

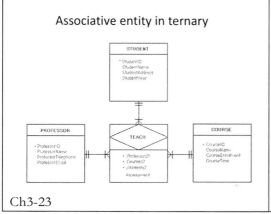

Ch3-23

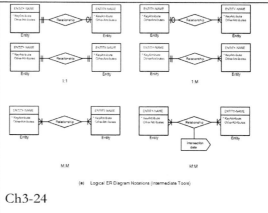

Ch3-24

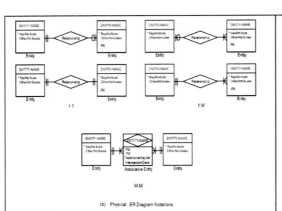

(b) Physical ER Diagram Notations

Ch3-25

Start Point (A) for ER Diagram: Transcript

- Transcript of the system (see an example in the textbook)
- (1) Identify entity and its attributes through identifying **noun**.
- (2) Identify relationship through identifying **verb** or verb phrase.
- (3) Identify cardinalities and modalities through identifying **business rules**.
- (4) Make commonsensical **assumptions** if the transcript does not provide all information you need.
- (5) Construct a short-version ERD for the case.
- (6) If there is an M:M relationship in your short-version ERD, convert the M:M relationship into 1:M relationships by adding an associative entity along with its intersection data attributes.
- (7) Complete the notations for all primary keys and foreign keys.

Ch3-26

Example of Transcript and the ERD

The School wants to create a database to maintain data for the school. Student data should include identification, name, address, and the earliest enrollment year. Professor data should include identification, name phone number, and office. Each professor has her/his own office, and teaches many courses each semester. Several professors might form a team to teach a single course. Each student can take many courses each semester. Course data should include unique course number, title, and enrollment cap. Each course can have its prerequisites. Each course must have a classroom. The school wants to keep track of students' grades.

Ch3-27

Ch3-28

Start Point (B) for ER Diagram: Sample Data Document

- Sample data documents (see an example in the textbook)
- (1) Identify the entities that have the attributes in the table.
- (2) Identify the relationships between the entities based on your understanding of the business environment.
- (3) Identify cardinalities and modalities based on commonsensical assumptions.
- (4) Construct a logical ERD for the case.
- (5) If there is an M:M relationship in your logical ERD, convert the M:M relationship into 1:M relationships by adding an associative entity along with its intersection data attributes.
- (6) Complete the notations for all primary keys and foreign keys.

Ch3-29

Figure 3.14. A Sample Datasheet for Construction of ER Diagram

Ch3-30

We will answer an important question
in Chapter 5

*Is there a criterion for judging whether
an ER diagram is correct or wrong?*

Ch3-31

Iterations of ER diagram construction

- Regardless whether the start point of an ER diagram is system descriptions or is sample datasheets, one-shot construction may not result in a good ER diagram.
- The construction of ER diagram and the normalization process should be carried out together.
- If a trial ER diagram is generated before the normalization process, this ER diagram might need to be revised after the normalization process to obtain the approved ER diagram for the database.
- If the start point is sample datasheets, one may perform the normalization process before constructing the trial ER diagram for the database. This fine point is illustrated in Technical Guide I through an example.

Ch3-32

Chapter 4.
Relational database

Ch4-1

Relational Data Model: Table

- In the relational data model, an entity is a relation, or a table.

Ch4-2

Properties of relation

- (1) The order of columns of a relation is not important

- (2) The order of row of a relation is not important

- (3) Each **cell** in the table can have only one single value. The value could be "**null**".

- (4) No two records in a relation have the same value of primary key.

Ch4-3

Candidate Key and Alternative Key

- A relation can have more than one attribute (or a combination of attributes) that can be used to identify the unique record in the table.

- For instance, if we assume StudentName (including first name, middle name, and last name) is unique in the database, then the STUDENT relation can have two **candidate keys**: StudentID and StudentName. If the DBA chooses StudentID to be the primary key for STUDENT, then StudentName is called the **alternative key**.

Ch4-4

Conversion of ER Model to Relational Data Model

(1) Constructing Tables
(2) Defining Constraints

Ch4-5

Constructing Tables

- It is a one seamless step procedure if our "standard" long-version ER diagram is used

- (1) An entity in the ER model is a relation in the relational data model

- (2) The primary key of an entity in the ER model is the primary key of the corresponding relation in the relational data model

- (3) The foreign key in an entity in the ER model is an attribute of the corresponding relation in the relational data model.

Ch4-6

242

Convert ERD to Relations

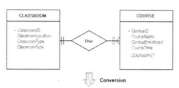

Ch4-7

Defining Constraints

- (1) For a relationship with 1:M cardinality, no constraint is needed as it is the default case.

- (2) For a relationship with 1:1 cardinality, define the constraint using the following pseudo-code:

  Table {CONSTRAINT *foreign-key* UNIQUE}

  For instance, for the 1:1 relationship between PROFESSOR and OFFICE in Figure 3.7, the constraint is

  PROFESSOR {CONSTRAINT *OfficeID* UNIQUE}

Ch4-8

Defining Constraints (cont'd)

- (3) For a relation with 1 modality, no constraint is needed as it is the default case. Nevertheless, the following pseudo-code can be used to make the default explicit.

  Table {CONSTRAINT MANDATORY TO} The-Other-Table

  For instance, in the Figure 3.7 example, the following constraint imposes 1 modality to the OFFICE table.

  OFFICE {CONSTRAINT MANDATORY TO} PROFESSOR

- (4) For a relation with 0 modality, define the constraint using the following pseudo-code.

  Table {CONSTRAINT OPTIONAL TO} The-Other-Table

  For instance, in the Figure 3.7 example, the following constraint imposes 0 modality to the PROFESSOR table.

  PROFESSOR {CONSTRAINT OPTIONAL TO} OFFICE

Ch4-9

Data Retrieval from Relational Database: Search-and-Match

(1) Massive B-trees in a large database to support direct access

(2) Simple cases: Data retrieval from a single table each time - Trace primary keys and foreign keys to find needed data

(3) Highly integrated data retrieval – Join multiple tables using keys and foreign keys of the tables

Ch4-10

Example: Simple data retrieval path

Find the assessment made by professor Fred Brown for student Chris Smith in the Database Design & Implementation course.

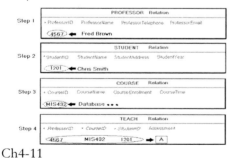

Ch4-11

Join operation

List course ID, course title, course enrollment, course time for each course along with its classroom's data including classroom ID, classroom type, classroom size.

It is impossible to retrieve needed data by using a simple data retrieval path.

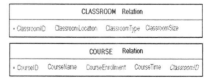

Ch4-12

243

Merged Table

COURSE-CLASSROOM

CourseID	CourseName	CourseEnrollment	CourseTime	ClassroomID	ClassroomLocation	ClassroomType	ClassroomSize
MIS212	Programming	40	MWF 9-10	T-001	T-Building	Comp-Lab	50
MIS432	Database	30	MWF 11-12	T-001	T-Building	Comp-Lab	50
ACT211	Accounting I	40	TR 10-11	L-213	L-Building	Lecture	60
FIN312	Finance	35	MWF 9-10	L-213	L-Building	Lecture	60
MGT211	Organization	38	TR 10-11	K-128	K-Building	Case-Room	40

Figure 4.5. Merge Tables through Join Operation

Ch4-13

Referential Integrity

- As the primary key in the 1-side table is the foreign key in the M-side table, there are potential violations of data integrity.
- For example, when the user deletes a classroom records but the classroom has already been assigned to several courses, what should the database do?
- The DBMS controls the data integrity based on rules

Ch4-14

Delete Rule:

- (1) **Restrict** – If there is a record in another table that is relating to the record to be deleted, the deletion is prohibited.

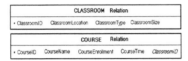

- A classroom record is allowed to be deleted only when it has not been assigned to any course.

Ch4-15

Delete Rule:

- (2) **Cascade** – All records in another table that are relating to the record to be deleted will be deleted as well.

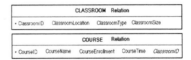

- If one deletes a classroom record, all records of the courses which use the classroom will be deleted automatically.

Ch4-16

Delete Rule:

- (3) **Set-to-Null** - All records in another table that are relating to the record to be deleted will be updated by setting the FK attribute to NULL.

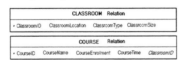

- If a classroom record is deleted, all courses that have been assigned to this classroom will be changed to "null" that means "no classroom".

Ch4-17

CHAPTER 5. NORMALIZATION AND LOGICAL DATABASE DESIGN

Ch5-1

Normalization

- **Normalization** is a process that evaluates the table structures and minimizes data redundancy.

Ch5-2

Functional Dependency

- **Functional dependency** defines the **determination relationships** between the attributes.
- The statement "*B is functionally dependent on A*" or "*A determines B*", where B is an attribute, A is an attribute or a group of attributes, means that "*if you know the value A, then you know the value of B.*"

  A → B

Ch5-3

Examples of functional dependency

- StudentID → StudentName
- [StudentID+CourseID] → Grade

Ch5-4

Functional Dependency

- The functional dependencies for a database are assumed by the database designer based on her/his conceptual understanding of the relationships between attributes in the real world.
- The functional dependencies for the database are usually objective "common sense", but can also be assumptions which may or may not be totally objective.

Ch5-5

Normal Form

- A **normal form** represents a certain type of functional dependency property of tables.
- We will emphasize on **first normal form (1NF)**, **second normal form (2NF)**, and **third normal form (3NF)**, although there are higher-level normal forms.
- Note that (1) if a table in 3NF, it must be also in 2NF; (2) if a table in 2NF, it must be in 1NF as well; (2) the database is in 3NF only if all tables are in 3NF.

Ch5-6

0NF

- A 0NF table has a missing value or multiple values in a cell, or has not primary key.

Student ID	Student Name	Course ID	Grade
1001	Chris Smith	ACT211	A
		MIS315	B
		MIS322	
10021	Anne Riley	ACT212	B
		MGT311	
		FIN312	A
10293	John Kerry	MGT212	B
		ACT211	A

Ch5-7

(b) Table with no primary key

Student ID	Student Name	Grade
10001	Chris Simth	A
10001	Chris Simth	B
10001	Chris Simth	B
10021	Anne Riley	B
10021	Anne Riley	A
10021	Anne Riley	A
10293	John Kerry	B
10293	John Kerry	A

Ch5-8

1NF

- A table is in **first normal form (1NF)** if it meets the following two conditions.
- (1) The table has no missing value or multiple values in a cell.
- (2) The primary key of the relation is identified based on assumptions of functional dependency among all attributes. These assumptions should be consistent with the **business rules** in the business environment.

Ch5-9

1NF

StudentID	StudentName	Major	Department	CourseID	CourseTitle	Grade
10003	John Smith	ACT	Accounting	ACT211	Fin Accouting	B
10003	John Smith	ACT	Accounting	ENG101	Intro English I	A
10014	Anne Gold	CHM	Chemistry	CHM101	Intro Chemistry	C
10014	Anne Gold	CHM	Chemistry	CHM291	Adv Chemistry	B
12343	Bob Brown	GNS	Biology	BIO101	Intro Biology	A
12343	Bob Brown	GNS	Biology	CHM101	Intro Chemistry	B
12343	Bob Brown	GNS	Biology	BIO345	Genetics II	A
13345	Mike Green	ACT	Accounting	ENG101	Intro English I	B
13345	Mike Green	ACT	Accounting	ENG201	Intro English II	B
13345	Mike Green	ACT	Accounting	ENG345	Literature	C

StudentID ········▶ StudentName
StudentID ········▶ Major
StudentID ········▶ Department
CourseID ········▶ CourseTitle
Major ········▶ Department
StudentID+CourseID ········▶ Grade

Ch5-10

Conversion from 0NF to 1NF

- **Step 1:** Eliminate missing values or repeating values in any cell.

- **Step 2:** Define all functional dependencies among the attributes based on the business environment or common sense. If there is an attribute without involving functional dependency (e.g., Grade in Figure 5.1(b)), you must create a functional dependency for it by adding a new attribute(s) (e.g., add CourseID for Grade in Figure 5.1(b)).

- **Step 3:** Identify the primary key for the table (e.g., [StudentID+CourseID] in Figure 5.2), so that if the value of the primary key is known then the value of any other attribute must be known.

Ch5-11

Problems with Tables in 1NF

- Data redundancies
- Modification anomalies
- The root of this problem is known as **partial key dependency**
- Student data depend on StudentID only (not [StudentID+CourseID])
- Course data depend on CourseID only (not [StudentID+CourseID]).

Ch5-12

Data modification anomaly

(1) Update anomaly

If a repeated fact is changed, all redundant values must be changed in each place they are stored.

(2) Insertion anomaly

A table with data redundancy could preclude useful facts.

(3) Deletion anomaly

A deletion of record from the table can cause unintentional deletion of facts.

Ch5-13

Decompose table in 1NF into tables in 2NF

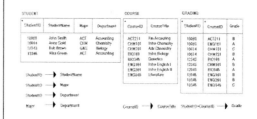

Ch5-14

Conversion from 1NF to 2NF

- **Step 1:** Make a list of potential individual keys derived from the primary key of the table in 1NF. For example, for the table in 1NF in Figure 5.2, thee potential individual keys can be derived from [StudentID+CourseID]; they are: StudentID, CourseID, and [StudentID+CourseID] itself.

- **Step 2:** For each attribute in the table in 1NF, assign it to the pertinent functionally dependent potential individual key. Using the example of Figure 5.2 and Figure 5.3, you can assign StudentName to StudentID, CourseTitle to CourseID, Grade to [StudentID+CourseID], and so on. The final result of the two steps is shown in Figure 5.4.

Ch5-15

Problems of tables in 2NF

- A table in 2NF can still contain data redundancy. For instance, the STUDENT table has repeating data of major and department.

- This problem is caused by **non-key dependency** (or **transitive dependency**); that is, the Major attribute is a non-key attribute, but it is the determinant of the Department attribute.

Ch5-16

Decompose table in 2NF into tables in 3NF

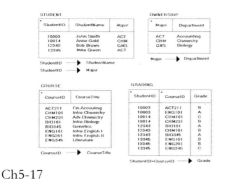

Ch5-17

Conversion from 2NF to 3NF

- **Step 1:** Identify any non-key dependency in the table in 2NF. In the example of Figure 5.4, Major → Department is a non-key dependency.
- **Step 2:** Create a new table (e.g., OWNERSHIP in the Figure 5.5 example) for the attributes involved in the non-key dependency (Major and Department in this example), and assign the primary key for this new table (Major in this example).
- **Step 3:** Keep the determinant attribute involved in the non-key dependency (Major in the Figure 5.5 example) in the original table (STUDENT) as the foreign key from the new table (OWNERSHIP), and delete other attributes involved in the non-key dependency (Department in this example) from the original table (STUDENT).

Ch5-18

The normalization procedure

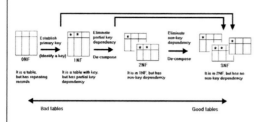

Ch5-19

Higher-level NF

- Tables in 3NF could still have data modification anomalies due to other types of functional dependencies.
- **BCNF (Boyce-Codd Normal Form)** addresses the "reverse" dependency problem in a 3NF table
- **4NF** addresses multivalued dependency problem.
- 5NF and domain-key normal form (DKNF) exist

Ch5-20

Requirements on Normalization

- The minimum requirements on normalization for tests would be 3NF in this course.
- There are assignments on the concepts of BCNF and 4NF. You are required to complete the assignments.
- Your course project of database design should meet 4NF.

Ch5-21

"Reverse" Dependency in Tables in 3NF

- "Reverse" dependency: a non-candidate-key attribute is the determinant of an attribute.
- This causes redundancy.

StudentID	Major	Advisor	MajorProject
10014	CHM	Brown	3.5
10014	GNS	Green	3.1
13345	ACT	Smith	3.2
12343	GNS	Green	3.7
13469	ACT	Jones	3.4

StudentID+Major ──▶ Advisor   Advisor ──▶ Major   ("Reverse" dependency)

StudentID+Major ──▶ MajorProject

Ch5-22

Decompose Table in 3NF into BCNF

STUDENT

StudentID	Advisor	MajorProject
10014	Brown	3.5
10014	Green	3.1
13345	Smith	3.2
12343	Green	3.7
13469	Jones	3.4

StudentID+Advisor ──▶ MajorProject

ADVISOR

Advisor	Major
Brown	CHM
Green	GNS
Smith	ACT
Jones	ACT

Advisor ──▶ Major

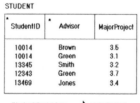

Ch5-23

Conversion from 3NF to BCNF

- **Step 1:** Identify any reverse dependency in the table in 3NF. In the example of Figure 5.7, Advisor → Major is a reverse dependency.
- **Step 2:** Create a new table (ADVISOR in the Figure 5.8 example) for the attributes involved in the reverse dependency (Advisor and Major in this example), and assign the primary key for this new table (Advisor in this example).
- **Step 3:** Make the determinant attribute involved in the reverse dependency (Advisor in the Figure 5.8 example) to be a part of the combination primary key of the original table (STUDENT), and delete other attributes involved in the reverse dependency (Major in this example) from the original table (STUDENT).

Ch5-24

Multivalued Dependency Problems of Tables in 3NF

- Multivalued dependency problem.
- For instance
- StudentID →→ Major

STUDENT

StudentID	StudentName	Major
10003	John Smith	ACT
10003	John Smith	FIN
10014	Anne Gold	CHM
12343	Bob Brown	GNS

StudentID ────→ StudentName
StudentID ──►► Major

- The STUDENT table might repeat the same facts.

Ch5-25

Decompose Table in 3NF into 4NF

STUDENT

StudentID	StudentName
10003	John Smith
10014	Anne Gold
12343	Bob Brown

MAJORS

StudentID	Major
10003	ACT
10003	FIN
10014	CHM
12343	GNS

StudentID ──→ StudentName   StudentID + Major ──►

Ch5-26

Conversion from 3NF to 4NF

- **Step 1:** Identify any multivalued dependency in the table in 3NF. In the example of Figure 5.9, StudentID →→ Major is a multivalued dependency.
- **Step 2:** Create a new table (e.g., MAJORS in the Figure 5.10 example) for the attributes involved in the multivalued dependency (StudentID and Major in this example), and assign the combination primary key for this new table ([StudentID+Major] in this example).
- **Step 3:** Delete the multivalued attribute involved in the multivalued dependency (Major in this example) from the original table (STUDENT).

Ch5-27

Logical Database Design

- **Logical database design** is the process that defines the databases structures to meet the data requirements of the business.
- **Step 1.** Generate an initial ER model
- **Step 2.** Convert the initial ER model into a preliminary set of tables.
- **Step 3.** Perform normalization on the preliminary set of tables into normalized tables (see the procedure in the previous section).
- **Step 4.** Revise the ER model based on the normalized tables.
- **Step 5.** Convert the normalized tables into the internal model for a selected DBMS.
- **Step 6.** Attach pertinent constraints to applicable tables.
- **Step 7.** Confirm that the internal model for the selected DBMS is consistent with the ER model.

Ch5-28

Three Important Points

- (1) The logical database design for a database is an iterative process. If the design process starts with data samples, Step 1 might be skipped, as explained in Technical Guide I.

- (2) The ERD of a database is a blueprint for the database. It is used for human communication. More importantly, because it is difficult for human to verify whether the computer internal model is consistent with those normalized tables without a blueprint, the ERD must be used. Technical Guide II shows more about this.

- (3) Logical database design ensures the data needs for the business, but does not take the performance of database into account. The ultimate consequence of data in higher-level normal forms is the inefficiency of data retrieval. To solve this problem in a large database, physical database design must be applied, as discussed in Chapter 7.

Ch5-29

Logical Database Design

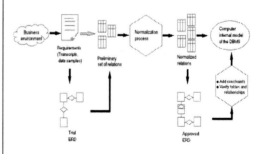

Ch5-30

CHAPTER 6. DATABASE PROCESSING
AND SQL

Ch6-1

SQL

- **SQL (Structured Query Language)** is a universal language for querying and updating databases.
- SQL integrates features of data definition languages (DDL) and data manipulation languages (DML).
- When using other computer languages (such as COBOL, C, Java, ADO.NET) to develop business process software that is connected to databases (Oracle, DB2, etc.), one must write SQL code

Ch6-2

SQL Examples

- The toy database for the examples

Ch6-3

```
CREATE TABLE tblStudent
  (StudentID CHAR(8),
   StudentName CHAR(20),
   StudentAddress CHAR(20),
   StudentEnrolYear INT,
   PRIMARY KEY (StudentID));
```

Listing 6.1. CREATE TABLE

Ch6-4

```
DROP TABLE tblStudent;
```

Listing 6.2. DROP TABLE

Ch6-5

```
INSERT INTO tblStudent
  VALUES ('01234567', 'John', '285
  Westport', 2012);
```

Listing 6.3. INSERT a Record

Ch6-6

250

```
UPDATE tblStudent
  SET StudentAddress = '300 Eastport'
  WHERE StudentID='01234567';
```

Listing 6.4. UPDATE a Record

Ch6-7

```
DELETE FROM tblStudent
  WHERE StudentID='01234567';
```

Listing 6.5. DELETE a Record

Ch6-8

Sample Data Used for Examples

StudentID	StudentName	StudentAddress	StudentEnrolYear
01234567	John	285 Westport	2012
02345678	Anne	287 Eastport	2014
03456789	Robert	324 Northport	2013

tblStudent

CourseID	CourseName	CourseEnroll
ACT211	Financial Accounting	35
ACT212	Cost Accounting	28
MIS315	Information Systems	40
MIS322	Systems Analysis & Design	38
MIS432	Database Design	30
MKT311	Principles of Marketing	25
MGT490	Special Topics	20

tblCourse

StudentID	CourseID	Grade
01234567	ACT211	A+
01234567	ACT212	A
01234567	MIS315	B
02345678	ACT211	B+
02345678	MIS322	C
03456789	ACT212	B
03456789	MIS432	A
03456789	MKT311	A

tblGrading

Ch6-9

*Find the student's name and address of student
ID 01234567 from the student table.*

```
SELECT StudentName,
StudentAddress
FROM tblStudent
WHERE StudentID = '01234567';
```

StudentName	StudentAddress
John	285 Westport

Listing 6.6. SELECT to Select Specified Data from a Table

Ch6-10

*Find the student's entire record of student ID
01234567 from the student table."*
The "*" sign represents all attributes of the table.

```
SELECT *
FROM tblStudent
WHERE StudentID = '01234567';
```

StudentID	StudentName	StudentAddress	StudentEnrolYear
01234567	John	285 Westport	2012

**Listing 6.7. SELECT to Select an Entire Record from a
Table**

Ch6-11

*Find distinctive student enrollment years
from the student table.*

```
SELECT DISTINCT StudentEnrolYear
  FROM tblStudent;
```

StudentEnrolYear
2012
2013
2014

Listing 6.8. DISTINCT to Eliminate Duplications

Ch6-12

251

List the names of those students who enroll to the program after 2011.

```
SELECT StudentName
FROM tblStudent
WHERE StudentEnrolYear > 2011;
```

Listing 6.9. Comparison - Greater Than

Ch6-13

List the names of those students whose ID numbers are greater than 00234567 and who enroll to the program after 2011 or before 2005.

```
SELECT StudentName
FROM tblStudent
WHERE StudentID > '00234567'
AND (StudentEnrolYear > 2011 OR
StudentEnrolYear < 2005);
```

StudentName
John
Anne
Robert

Listing 6.10. AND and OR Operators

Ch6-14

Find the student records for those students whose street names contain 'Westport'.

Here, the percent sign "%" is a wildcard to represent any collection of characters. Note that, Microsoft Access uses "*" for this type of wildcard.

```
SELECT *
FROM tblStudent
WHERE StudentAddress LIKE '%Westport%';
```

StudentID	StudentName	StudentAddress	StudentEnrolYear
01234567	John	285 Westport	2012

Listing 6.11. LIKE Operator and Wildcard "%"

Ch6-15

Find the student record for each student whose name has the letter 'o' as the second letter of the name.

Here, the wildcard sign "_" represents any one character. Note that, Microsoft Access uses "?" for this type of wildcard.

```
SELECT *
FROM tblStudent
WH
```

StudentID	StudentName	StudentAddress	StudentEnrolYear
01234567	John	285 Westport	2012
03456789	Robert	324 Northport	2013

Listing 6.12. LIKE Operator and Wildcard "_"

Ch6-16

Find the student whose ID is '01234567', '00234567', or '00034567'.

```
SELECT StudentName
FROM tblStudent
WHERE StudentID IN ('01234567',
'00234567', '00034567');
```

StudentName
John

Listing 6.13. IN Operator

Ch6-17

SQL-User Interaction

- SQL is mainly embedded in host computer programming languages (C++, Java, .NET, COBOL...)
- SQL can be used on PC and includes user input request, depending on versions.
- For example:

```
SELECT StudentName
FROM tblStudent
WHERE StudentID=[Please input student ID:];
```

Ch6-18

List all student records in the reverse alphabetic order by student name.

```
SELECT *
FROM tblStudent
ORDER BY StudentName DESC;
```

StudentID	StudentName	StudentAddress	StudentEnrolYear
03456789	Robert	324 Northport	2013
01234567	John	285 Westport	2012
02345678	Anne	287 Eastport	2014

Listing 6.14. ORDER BY Clause

Ch6-19

Find the total student records in the student table.

```
SELECT COUNT(*)
FROM tblStudent;
```

Expr1000
3

Listing 6.15(a). COUNT Function

Ch6-20

Find the total student records in the student table.

```
SELECT COUNT(*) AS CountOfStudents
FROM tblStudent;
```

CountOfStudents
3

Listing 6.15(b). Use AS Keyword to Define Result Name

Ch6-21

What are the smallest enrollment number, largest enrollment number, total enrollment number, and average enrollment number in the course table?

```
SELECT MIN(CourseEnrollment),
       MAX(CourseEnrollment),
       SUM(CourseEnrollment),
       AVG(CourseEnrollment)
FROM tblCourse;
```

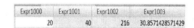

Expr1000	Expr1001	Expr1002	Expr1003
20	40	216	30.8571428571429

Listing 6.16. MIN, MAX, SUM, and AVG Functions

Ch6-22

Find the total number of courses taken by **each** student, and only include students who have taken at least 2 courses."

```
SELECT StudentID, COUNT(*)
FROM tblGrading
GROUP BY StudentID
HAVING COUNT(*) > 1;
```

StudentID	Expr1001
01234567	3
02345678	2
03456789	3

Listing 6.17. GROUP BY Clause and HAVING Clause

Ch6-23

List the names of those students who receive "A" or "A+" in any course.

```
SELECT DISTINCT tblStudent.StudentName
FROM tblGrading, tblStudent
WHERE
tblStudent.StudentID=tblGrading.StudentID
AND (tblGrading.Grade='A+' OR
     tblGrading.Grade='A');
```

StudentID	Expr1001
02345678	2
03456789	3

Listing 6.18. Join Two Tables

Ch6-24

Rules of Join

- (1) A condition associates two tables, and the general format is:

  [*TableOnOneSide*].[*PrimaryKey*] = [*TableOnManySide*].[*ForeignKey*]

- (2) If *n* tables are used in the query, then *n*-1 conditions are needed and are tied by the AND operator.

- (3) To differentiate the same names in different tables, the table name followed by a period sign is used for an attribute name (e.g., tblStudent.StudentID) to **qualify** the attribute name. In other words, the table name must be quoted to specify what table the attribute belongs to.

Ch6-25

- *List the names of those students who receive "A" or "A+" in any course.*

```
SELECT DISTINCT tblStudent.StudentName
FROM tblGrading, tblStudent
WHERE
    tblStudent.StudentID=tblGrading.StudentID
    AND (tblGrading.Grade='A+' OR
    tblGrading.Grade='A');
```

Listing 6.19. Join Two Tables

StudentName
John
Robert

Ch6-26

```
SELECT *
FROM tblStudent, tblCourse, tblGrading
WHERE tblStudent.StudentID = tblGrading.StudentID
AND tblCourse.CourseID = tblGrading.CourseID;
```

Listing 6.20. Join Multiple Tables to Integrate Related Data

Ch6-27

Who (student ID and name) receives "A+" or "A" grade in which course (course ID and course name)? List the results in order of student ID.

```
SELECT tblGrading.StudentID, tblStudent.StudentName,
tblGrading.CourseID, tblCourse.CourseName,
tblGrading.Grade
FROM tblGrading, tblStudent, tblCourse
WHERE tblStudent.StudentID=tblGrading.StudentID
AND tblCourse.CourseID=tblGrading.CourseID
AND (tblGrading.Grade='A+' OR tblGrading.Grade='A')
ORDER BY tblStudent.StudentID;
```

StudentID	StudentName	CourseID	CourseName	Grade
01234567	John	ACT212	Cost Accounting	A
01234567	John	ACT211	Financial Accounting	A+
05456789	Eleven	MKT311	Principles of Marketing	A
09456789	Robert	MIS432	Database Design	A

Listing 6.21. Query with Multiple Table

Ch6-28

```
SELECT DISTINCT tblStudent.StudentName
FROM tblStudent
INNER JOIN tblGrading
ON
tblStudent.StudentID=tblGrading.StudentID
WHERE (tblGrading.Grade='A+' OR
        tblGrading.Grade='A');
```

Listing 6.22. Explicit Format of Inner Join

This format is not recommended for beginners.

Ch6-29

Outer Join (-outer join is not used often)

List the course ID and course name for all grades. Include all courses in the results. For courses that do not have grade records, omit the grade.

```
SELECT tblCourse.CourseID, tblCourse.CourseName,
    tblGrading.Grade
FROM tblCourse LEFT JOIN tblGrading
    ON tblCourse.CourseID=tblGrading.CourseID;
```

Listing 6.23. Query with Left Outer Join Clause

CourseID	CourseName	Grade
MIS315	Information Systems	B
MIS272	Systems Analysis & Design	C
ACT211	Financial Accounting	A+
ACT211	Financial Accounting	B-
MKT311	Principles of Marketing	A
ACT212	Cost Accounting	B
ACT212	Cost Accounting	A
MIS432	Database Design	A
MGT490	Special Topics	

Ch6-30

Subquery

- Alternative to join operation for special cases

```
SELECT tblStudent.StudentName
FROM    tblStudent
WHERE   tblStudent.StudentID IN
         (SELECT tblGrading.StudentID
          FROM tblGrading
          WHERE(tblGrading.Grade='A+'
          OR tblGrading.Grade='A'));
```

StudentName
John
Robert

Listing 6.24. An Example of Subquery that Avoids Join Operation

Ch6-31

Subquery

- An alternative to the GROUP BY clause.

Show each student's name along with the number of courses she/he has taken.

```
SELECT tblStudent.StudentName,
    (SELECT COUNT(*)
     FROM tblGrading
     WHERE
     tblStudent.StudentID=tblGrading.StudentID)
     AS NumberOfCourses
FROM tblStudent;
```

StudentName	NumberOfCourses
John	3
Anne	2
Robert	3

Listing 6.25(a). Subquery for Groups

Ch6-32

GROUP BY seems to be easier

The SQL in Listing 6.25(a) does the similar work as GROUP BY clause

```
SELECT tblStudent.StudentName,
    COUNT(*) AS NumberOfCourses
FROM tblStudent, tblGrading
WHERE
tblStudent.StudentID=tblGrading.StudentID
GROUP BY tblStudent.StudentName;
```

Listing 6.25(b). GROUP BY for Group

Ch6-33

Subquery

- Determine uncertain criteria

Which students with ID numbers greater than '02000000' have the earliest enrollment year of such students?

```
SELECT StudentName
FROM    tblStudent
WHERE   StudentID > '02000000'
AND StudentEnrolYear=
     (SELECT MIN(StudentEnrolYear)
      FROM tblStudent
      WHERE  StudentID > '02000000');
```

StudentName
Robert

Listing 6.26. An Example of Subquery for Uncertain Condition

Ch6-34

List student names, course names, and grades of those students whose ID numbers are greater than '02000000' and have the earliest enrollment year of such students.

```
SELECT tblStudent.StudentName,
    tblCourse.CourseName,       tblGrading.Grade
FROM tblStudent, tblCourse, tblGrading
WHERE tblStudent.StudentID=tblGrading.StudentID
AND tblCourse.CourseID=tblGrading.CourseID
AND tblStudent.StudentID > '02000000'
AND tblStudent.StudentEnrolYear=
    (SELECT MIN(tblStudent.StudentEnrolYear)
     FROM tblStudent
     WHERE  tblStudent.StudentID > '02000000');
```

StudentName	CourseName	Grade
Robert	Database Design	A
Robert	Cost Accounting	B
Robert	Principles of Marketing	A

Listing 6.27. An Example of Join and Subquery

Ch6-35

Rules of Subquery

- First, when the right side of the WHERE clause is uncertain (e.g., MIN, MAX, SUM, AVG, COUNT), you must use a subquery to replace the uncertain condition.
- Second, in Listing 6.24, you can see that the condition StudentID>'02000000' in the host WHERE clause repeats in the condition in the subquery. If the second WEHRE clause is omitted, the query is quite different from the original meaning, and stands for *"which students with ID numbers greater than '02000000' have the earliest enrollment year of all students?"*

Ch6-36

UNION Operator

List the course ID and course enrollment for each course that has enrollment greater than 35, or the student name and student ID for each student who enrolled after 2013.

```
SELECT CourseID AS Name, CourseEnrollment AS Data
FROM tblCourse
WHERE CourseEnrollment>35
UNION
SELECT StudentName AS Name, StudentID AS Data
FROM tblStudent
WHERE StudentEnrolYear>2013;
```

Name	Data
Anne	02345678
MIS315	40
MIS322	38

Figure 6.28. UNION Operator

(This example is merely to demonstrate how the UNION operator works. The query result is a kind of "orange" and "apple".)

Ch6-37

Tactics for Writing Queries

- (1) Read the query carefully. Determine what data are to be retrieved and what attributes are to be included in the SELECT command.
- (2) Determine what tables are will be used in the FROM clause.
- (3) If two or more tables are involved, use join operation in the WHERE clause. Do not use aggregate function in WHERE clause directly.
- (4) Construct the WHERE clause by including all conditions that are linked by AND or OR.
- (5) If a condition has an uncertain criterion (MAX, MIN, AVG, SUM, COUNT) on the right side of the condition, use subquery.

Ch6-38

SQL Embedded in Host Computer Programming Languages

- Computer application programs in large languages (e.g., COBOL, C++, Java, and .NET) often deal with relational databases directly and host SQL script. To make a connection to the databases and process the embedded SQL, specific database connection software must be integrated into the system.

- (We have a demo of ASP.NET. You may take an elective course to learn more about server-side programming for Web application development.)

Ch6-39

Search Access Database in the Internet Environment - An Example of ADO.NET

Ch6-40

CHAPTER 7. PHYSICAL DATABASE DESIGN

Ch7-1

Physical Design

- **Physical database design** is to alter the logical database design and improve the database performance

- **Response time** – the time delay from the database access request to the result appears;
- **Throughput volume** – the data access output in a given time period;
- **Security** – the data protection.

Ch7-2

Physical Database Design Techniques

- Unlike logical database design, physical database design is more or less artistic and depends upon the specific situations of applications of the database.
- The support functions for physical design vary depending on the DBMS. Large DBMS such as Oracle and DB2 have rich functionalities for physical database design, but end user oriented DBMS for tiny databases, such as Microsoft Access, have few physical design features.
- We discuss 10 physical database design techniques

Ch7-3

Adding Index

- For example, if the user finds students from the STUDENT table often by StudentName, then StudentName should have an index although it is not the primary key.

- The downside of adding indexes is the increase of computation overhead for maintenance of B-trees.

Ch7-4

Adding Subschema

Students' Subschema   Professors' Subschema   Bursar's Subschema

Tables of Database

Ch7-5

Clustering Tables

- If two or more tables are used together so often, these tables should be **clustered**; that is, are placed close each to other (e.g., on the same disk cylinder).

- The downside of clustering is that it might increase the "distances" between one of the clustered table and other tables because not all tables can be clustered.

Ch7-6

Merging Tables

- If two or more tables are repeatedly joined through the join operations, then **merging** these tables into a large table might be necessary to reduce the valuable computing time spent on the repeating join operations.
- The **combined table** becomes a **denormalized** table and usually contains data redundancy.
- To keep the data sufficiently accurate, re-merging could take place from time to time.

Ch7-7

Horizontal Partitioning Table

- In **horizontal partitioning**, the rows of a table are divided into parts, and the parts are stored separately for many reasons, such as different access frequencies of the parts and different security requirement of the parts.
- For instance, if the STUDENT table is huge, it can be divided into two parts: one sub-table contains records of active students and the other sub-table contains records of inactive students.
- The downside of partitioning is that the computation overhead would be increase when the entire table is used.

Ch7-8

Horizontal partitioning

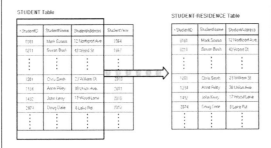

Ch7-9

Vertical Partitioning Table

- In **vertical partitioning**, the columns of a table are divided into parts, and the parts are stored separately because different users require different attributes.
- For instance, if the STUDENT table is huge, it can be divided into two parts: one sub-table contains attributes StudentID, StudentName, and StudentYear; and the other sub-table contains attributes StudentID, StudentName, and StudentAddress.
- The concepts of vertical partitioning and adding indexes are different.

Ch7-10

Vertical Partitioning

Ch7-11

Creating New Primary Key

- Combination primary keys make data retrieval process slower, especially when the combination key involves too many attributes, because it makes too many indexed attributes in the B-trees.

Ch7-12

Substituting Foreign Key

- If an alternative key of the table on the 1-side is more often used for data retrieval than the primary key, this alternative key could be used as the foreign key of the table on the M-side.
- For instance, in the database represented by Figure 3.9, considering ProfessorName is an alternative key of the PROFESSOR relation, and is used more frequently than ProfessorID, *ProfessorName* can substitute *ProfessorID* as the foreign key in the TEACH relation.

Ch7-13

Duplicating Table or Parts of Partitioned Table

- When multiple users try to access the same table, the response time of the database will slow. To reduce the bottleneck effect, the technique of **duplicating tables** (or parts of partitioned tables) is used at the risk of overt data redundancy.
- The duplication should be temporary for the access peak hours, and should be fully managed by the DBMS.

Ch7-14

Storing Information (Processd Data)

- If a piece of information (or processed data, e.g., total) is requested frequently and/or by many users in a short period, the system would waste much computation resource.
- **Storing** information is to reduce the unnecessarily repeating computation.
- Apparently, the stored piece of information should be of short life to keep the information updated.

Ch7-15

Implementation of Physical Database Design

- The implementation of physical database design highly depends on the DBMS.

- (1) **Storage-related construction.**
- (2) **SQL-related construction.** SQL allows the user of the database to create VIEW. This makes it possible to create a VIEW of multiple tables for security, or to create partitions of a single table.
- (3) **Query optimizer.** Many DBMSs support SQL ANALYZE command to analyze database performance statistics. A DBMS has its own algorithms for determine the most efficient way to execute SQL.

Ch7-16

CHAPTER 8. DATABASE ADMINISTRATION

Ch8-1

DBA Responsibilities

- Data Planning and Database Design
- Data Coordination
- Data Security, Access Policies, and Data Ownership
- Data Quality
- Database Performance
- User Training
- Data Standards, Data Dictionary, and Documentation
- Database Backup and Recovery
- Data Archiving
- Database Maintenance
- Managing Business Rules

Ch8-2

Data Quality:
Data quality is evaluated by

- accuracy
- objectivity
- believability
- reputation
- access
- security
- relevancy
- value-added
- timeliness
- completeness
- amount of data
- interpretability
- ease of understanding
- concise representation
- consistent representation.

Ch8-3

Data Dictionary

- A data dictionary stores **metadata**, namely data about the data in the database.
- There is no universal standard for data dictionary. Individual DBMS has the data dictionary in its own way.
- A **passive data dictionary** is used for **documentation** purposes.
- An **active data dictionary** is a sophisticated one that interacts with the "mother database" in a real-time fashion.

Ch8-4

Simple Example of
Data Dictionary

"Mother Database"

CLASSROOM	Relation		
• ClassroomID	ClassroomLocation	ClassroomType	ClassroomSize

COURSE	Relation			
• CourseID	CourseName	CourseEnrollment	CourseTime	ClassroomID

Data Dictionary

Relations Metadata

Table Name	Number of Records	Disk Cylinder	Access Permission code
CLASSROOM	232	AC54	193
COURSE	568	M487	347

Attributes Metadata

Attribute Name	Data Type	Attribute Length	Indexed	Validation Rule Code
ClassroomID	Text	6	Key / PI	12
ClassroomLocation	Text	10	No	23
ClassroomType	Text	10	No	28
ClassroomSize	Number	3	No	36
CourseID	Text	6	Key	12
CourseName	Text	10	Yes	28
CourseEnrollment	Number	3	No	36
CourseTime	Date/Time	10	No	11

Ch8-5

Learn Data Dictionary from Your Microsoft Access Project

- Following Technical Guide II for using Microsoft Access, you can find a way to retrieve the DMBS generated data dictionary for the database in Microsoft Access. If you build a database for your course project, you can learn a variety of metadata that are useful for database management.

[Demo Data Dictionary in Microsoft Access]

Ch8-6

Backup and Recovery Approaches

- Mirrored databases – Too expensive
- Re-do transactions – for a large scale disaster
- Un-do transactions – for a small scale error

Ch8-7

Re-Do Transactions

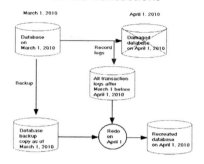

Ch8-8

Un-Do Transactions

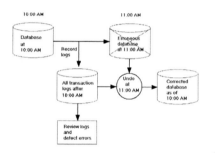

Ch8-9

Data Archiving

- Special needs for data retention
- Business laws and government laws requirements for data retention
- Data archive is a place where a set of certain data stored
- Data archive does not belong to the database, but should be traceable from the database

Ch8-10

Database Maintenance

- Hardware and software upgrading
- Other changes in the environment.
- Long-term maintenance policies
- Short-term maintenance plans
- The responsibility of dealing with cost issues and the relationships with vendors

Ch8-11

Managing Business Rules

- A **business rule** is a statement that aims to influence or guide business in the organization.
- Business rules include business regulation, organization structure, job responsibility, business procedure, security, database, and others.
- One of the DBA roles is to manage the business rules related to the database design.
- (1) Functional dependencies between the attributes of entities.
- (2) Cardinalities and modalities attached to the relationships between the entities.
- (3) Referential integrity rules for record insertion and deletion

Ch8-12

CHAPTER 9. DATABASE IN COMPUTER NETWORKS Ch9-1	**Centralized Database in the Local Area Network Environment** 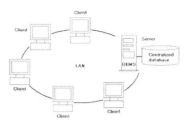 Ch9-2
Centralized Database in the Internet Environment 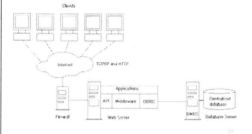 Ch9-3	**ODBC – An important component**  Ch9-4
Distributed Database 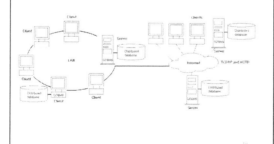 Ch9-5	**Distributed Database** • Location transparency - The DDBMS takes care of data physical locations and data migration, and makes the users feel the database is centralized in somewhere. • Data deployment • (1) **Partitioning** – A table may be split up through **horizontal partitioning**, **vertical partitioning**, or the combination of horizontal and vertical partitioning, and each **fragment** is subject to placement. • (2) **Placement** – A table or a fragment of table should be placed at the site where the table or the fragment is used most frequently, and the site takes the major responsibility for its data integrity control as well as backup and recovery. • (3) **Duplication** – A table or a fragment of table may have a replicated copy at the site where the table is used frequently. Ch9-6

Example of data deployment

- Given the situation described in the textbook of the database:

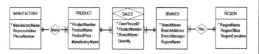

- There are headquarter (Boston) and 4 region offices

Ch9-7

Situations

- *GreenAppliance retail company has the database as described in Figure 9.5(a).*
- *Its headquarters is set in Boston.*
- *There are four region offices: Providence, Toronto, New York, and Seattle.*
- *Each region office manages dozens branches in the region. Each region sells unique products.*

Ch9-8

Situations (cont'd)

- *The CEOs of the company monitor the sales across the company on the daily basis, and also make decisions on the selection of suppliers regularly.*
- *The senior managers of each region office take the responsibility of sales and the performance of its branches, but do not deal with the suppliers directly.*
- *What is your strategy of deployment of the tables for the distributed database?*

Ch9-9

Data Deployment Matrix

Location / Tables	Headquarters Boston	Region Offices Toronto, Miami, Seattle, Providence
MANUFACTORY	The table is placed in Boston.	
BRANCH	The table is placed in Boston.	
REGION	The table is placed in Boston.	
PRODUCT	The table is placed in Boston.	A duplicated horizontally partitioned part is placed in each region. The H.P. is based on the values of ProductNumber that are related to the region through SALES and BRANCH.
SALES	A duplicated table is placed in Boston which merges the four segments of the horizontally partitioned parts of the four regions.	A horizontally partitioned part is placed in each region. The H.P. is based on the values of BranchName that are related to the region through BRANCH.

Ch9-10

Data deployment Graph

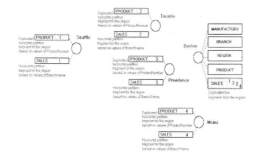

Ch9-11

Justification

- (1) The REGION and BRANCH tables are mainly used by the headquarters and are rarely used by any region office. Thus, these two tables are placed in Boston.
- (2) As the headquarters makes decisions on suppliers, the MANUFACTORY table is placed in Boston. Region offices might access the MANUFACTORY table occasionally, but the usage is low since they do not assume the responsibility of selection of suppliers.

Ch9-12

Justification (cont'd)

- (3) As each region office takes the responsibility of sales and its performance, the SALES table should be horizontally partitioned for each region office. The individual sub-table is placed to the corresponding region office. The headquarters also needs to access the SALES table on the daily basis but not in the real-time mode. Thus, a duplication SALES table, which merges the four sub-tables of the four region offices, is placed in Boston.

- (4) As the headquarters takes the responsibility of selection of suppliers, the PRODUCT table is placed in Boston. However, each region office must access the PRODUCT table as well for monitoring sales activities. As each region sells unique products, the PRODUCT table is duplicated for each region office for only a horizontally partitioned part which is relevant to the products for that region.

Ch9-13

Distributed Database

- Data integrity control

- Distributed join operations - Join operations in distributed databases would become more time consuming because the joined tables may not be located in the same place. Many heuristic algorithms are employed to "optimize" **distributed join operations**.

Ch9-14

Interfaces of Databases

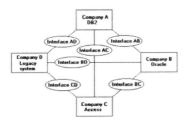

Ch9-15

XML for databases

Ch9-16

XML

- The XML data model is hierarchical, not relational. The conversion of data from a relational database into the XML format might not be straightforward.

- The use of XML involves several companion tools, such as XSLT or CSS, XML Schema or DDT, and is not as simple as it should be.

Ch9-17

Example of XML

```
<?xml version="1.0" standalone="yes"?>
<StudentTable>
  <Student
        StudentID="01234567"
        StudentName="John"
        StudentAddress="285 Westport"
        StudentEnrolYear="2012" >
  </Student>
  <Student
        StudentID="02345678"
        StudentName="Anne"
        StudentAddress="287 Eastport"
        StudentEnrolYear="2014" >
  </Student>
  <Student
        StudentID="03456789"
        StudentName="Robert"
        StudentAddress="324 Northport"
        StudentEnrolYear="2013" >
  </Student>
</StudentTable>
```

Listing 9.1. XML Document for the STUDENT Table in Figure 6.2

Ch9-18

CHAPTER 10. DATA WAREHOUSE AND DATA MINING

Ch10-1

Data Warehouse

- In a large organization, it is unlikely to have just one database.
- People need a variety of types of data which may not be normalized or may not be current.
- A **Data warehouse** holds all kinds of data for supporting decision making activities.
- A data warehouse can be divided into **data marts**, and each data mart serves a particular functional division (e.g., finance, accounting, human resource management, etc.).
- **High-dimensional** data

Ch10-2

Multidimensional Data and data Cube

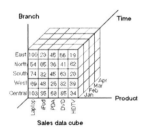

Sales data cube

Ch10-3

Creating Data Cube from Relational Database: Star Schema

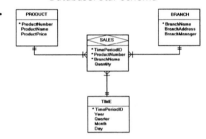

Star Schema for Generating High-dimensional Data Cube

Ch10-4

Star Schema

- The **fact table** is the center of the star, and is SALES table in this example that keeps sales data for the data cube.
- The query *"Find all monthly sales which are generated by every branch for every existing product within the past four months"* will generate a sales data cube.

Ch10-5

Snowflake Design

Snowflake design is 1:M relationship chains towards the center of the star

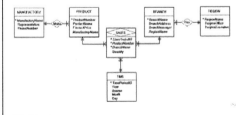

Ch10-6

Snowflake Design

- **Snowflake design** is an extension of star schema design of multidimensional data for data warehousing.
- Since the relationships between tables are always 1:M towards the fact table, the snowflake design makes meaningful very high dimensional data cubes possible.

Ch10-7

OLAP

- **OLAP** (Online Analytical Processing) is one of the most popular business intelligence techniques in organizations.
- The word **"online"** means data availability.

Ch10-8

Tactics of OLAP

- Query
- **Slicing** is to reduce the dimensionality of data by fixing the level(s) of one or more dimensions to create **slices**.
- **Dicing** is to divide the data cube into sub-cubes (so called **dice**) for comparison, (e.g., actual vs. plan, this year vs. last year).
- Combinations of slicing and dicing with other methods (such as queries) are also called **drill-down**, which means investigating information in increasing details.

Ch10-9

Slicing

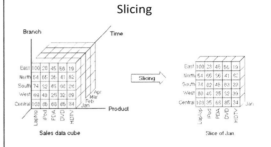

Ch10-10

Dicing

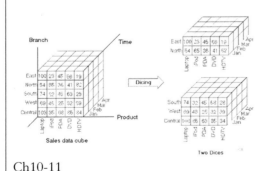

Ch10-11

Business Intelligence and Data Mining

- **Business intelligence** is a broad category of applications and technologies of gathering, accessing, and analyzing a large amount of data for the organization to make effective business decisions.
- Data mining is the process of trawling through data in the hope of identifying patterns.

Ch10-12

A Data Mining Story

- There is a well-known supermarket data mining story that *consumers who purchase diaper are more likely to purchase beer at the same time.*
- This story sounds interesting because such a purchase pattern is unsuspected.
- Apparently, these consumers may not be the typical ones. This story is an example to demonstrate to people how data mining could help the business to catch opportunities although such an unsuspected fact might be regional or short-lived.

Ch10-13

Closing Episode

Ch10-14

CPSIA information can be obtained at www.ICGtesting.com
Printed in the USA
BVOW021733011212

307026BV00005B/40/P